WITHDRAWN
PRACTICAL
SOCIAL WORK

Series Editor: Jo Campling

BASW

Social work is at an important stage in its development. All professions must be responsive to changing social and economic conditions if they are to meet the needs of those they serve. This series focuses on sound practice and the specific contribution which social workers can make to the well-being of our society.

The British Association of Social Workers has always been conscious of its role in setting guidelines for practice and in seeking to raise professional standards. The conception of the Practical Social Work series arose from a survey of BASW members to discover where they, the practitioners in social work, felt there was the most need for new literature. The response was overwhelming and enthusiastic, and the result is a carefully planned, coherent series of books. The emphasis is firmly on practice set in a theoretical framework. The books will inform, stimulate and promote discussion, thus adding to the further development of skills and high professional standards. All the authors are practitioners and teachers of social work representing a wide variety of experience.

JO CAMPLING

A list of published titles in this series follows overleaf

Practical Social Work
Series Standing Order ISBN 0–333–69347–7

You can receive future titles in this series as they are published by placing a standing order. Please contact your bookseller or, in the case of difficulty, write to us at the address below with your name and address, the title of the series and the ISBN quoted above.

Customer Services Department, Macmillan Distribution Ltd
Houndmills, Basingstoke, Ham~~

D0543065

PRACTICAL SOCIAL WORK

Robert Adams *Social Work and Empowerment*

David Anderson *Social Work and Mental Handicap*

Sarah Banks *Ethics and Values in Social Work (2nd edn)*

James G. Barber *Beyond Casework*

James G. Barber *Social Work with Addictions*

Peter Beresford and Suzy Croft *Citizen Involvement*

Suzy Braye and Michael Preston-Shoot *Practising Social Work Law (2nd edn)*

Robert Brown, Stanley Bute and Peter Ford *Social Workers at Risk*

Helen Cosis Brown *Social Work and Sexuality*

Alan Butler and Colin Pritchard *Social Work and Mental Illness*

Crescy Cannan, Lynne Berry and Karen Lyons *Social Work and Europe*

Roger Clough *Residential Work*

David M. Cooper and David Ball *Social Work and Child Abuse*

Veronica Coulshed and Audrey Mullender *Management in Social Work (2nd edn)*

Veronica Coulshed and Joan Orme *Social Work Practice: An Introduction (3rd edn)*

Paul Daniel and John Wheeler *Social Work and Local Politics*

Peter R. Day *Sociology in Social Work Practice*

Lena Dominelli *Anti-Racist Social Work (2nd edn)*

Celia Doyle *Working with Abused Children (2nd edn)*

Angela Everitt and Pauline Hardiker *Evaluating for Good Practice*

Angela Everitt, Pauline Hardiker, Jane Littlewood and Audrey Mullender *Applied Research for Better Practice*

Kathy Ford and Alan Jones *Student Supervision*

David Francis and Paul Henderson *Working with Rural Communities*

Michael D.A. Freeman *Children, their Families and the Law*

Alison Froggatt *Family Work with Elderly People*

Danya Glaser and Stephen Frosh *Child Sexual Abuse (2nd edn)*

Gill Gorell Barnes *Working with Families*

Cordelia Grimwood and Ruth Popplestone *Women, Management and Care*

Jalna Hanmer and Daphne Statham *Women and Social Work*

Tony Jeffs and Mark Smith (eds) *Youth Work*

Michael Kerfoot and Alan Butler *Problems of Childhood and Adolescence*

Joyce Lishman *Communication in Social Work*

Carol Lupton and Terry Gillespie (eds) *Working with Violence*

Mary Marshall and Mary Dixon *Social Work with Older People (3rd edn)*

Paula Nicolson and Rowan bayne *Applied Psychology for Social Workers (2nd edn)*

Kieran O'Hagan *Crisis Intervention in Social Services*

Michael Oliver and Bob Sapey *Social Work with Disabled People (2nd edn)*

Joan Orme and Bryan Glastonbury *Care Management*

Malcolm Payne *Working in Teams*

John Pitts *Working with Young Offenders (2nd end)*

Michael Preston-Shoot *Effective Groupwork*

Peter Raynor, David Smith and Maurice Vanstone *Effective Probation Practice*

Steven Shardlow and Mark Doel *Practice Learning and Teaching*

Carole R. Smith *Social Work with the Dying and Bereaved*

David Smith *Criminology for Social Work*

Gill Stewart and John Stewart *Social Work and Housing*

Christine Stones *Focus on Families*

Neil Thompson *Anti-Discriminatory Practice (3rd edn)*

Neil Thompson, Michael Murphy and Steve Stradling *Dealing with Stress*

Derek Tilbury *Working with Mental Illness (2nd edn)*

Alan Twelvetrees *Community Work (3rd edn)*

Hilary Walker and Bill Beaumont (eds) *Working with Offenders*

Working with Mental Illness

A Community-based Approach

Second Edition

Derek Tilbury

palgrave

First edition 1993
Reprinted four times
Second edition 2002

Published by
PALGRAVE
Houndmills, Basingstoke, Hampshire RG21 6XS and
175 Fifth Avenue, New York, N. Y. 10010
Companies and representatives throughout the world

PALGRAVE is the new global academic imprint of St. Martin's Press LLC Scholarly and Reference Division and Palgrave Publishers Ltd (formerly Macmillan Press Ltd).

ISBN 0–333–94733–9

This book is printed on paper suitable for recycling and made from fully managed and sustained forest sources.

A catalogue record for this book is available from the British Library.

10   9   8   7   6   5   4   3   2   1
11 10 09 08 07 06 05 04 03 02

Printed in China

HV
689
T54
2002

Contents

List of Figures

Preface

This book, like many others, is a synthesis, emerging from my training and practice as a psychiatric social worker, my involvement with voluntary organisations (mainly Mind) and my teaching of social work theory and mental health to social work students over the years, together with all the associated reading. In addition to other authors, then, I am indebted to my mentors, to my colleagues from a wide variety of professional and academic backgrounds, to fellow voluntary workers, to my students, their practice teachers and agencies, but, above all, to my former clients and their families. I hope they feel that, in the end, they managed to teach me something.

The first edition of this book focused on the fundamentals of practice involving mental illness. This second edition has the same focus, but changes in the context of practice are bound to have an influence. The intervening years have seen very considerable shifts in the field of mental health policy. It is now high on the political agenda; a priority target area for the NHS, with local services under central government pressures to integrate health and local authority provisions to meet national standards and involve users' and carers' representatives in service planning and delivery. Major concerns include the combating of the social exclusion experienced by those suffering from mental illness, more choice in and control over treatments, the provision of culturally sensitive services reflecting a multicultural society, an extension of concerns for civil liberties and human rights through the growth of advocacy, and proposals for independent tribunals to determine longer detention but at the same time extending the use of compulsion into community settings. Public protection now figures prominently, with issues around how to deal with severe personality disorder. I have endeavoured to identify where these more recent developments impinge on practice. Most will be welcomed, some give rise to questions.

DEREK TILBURY

Introduction

For the purposes of this book it is assumed that readers will be familiar with the principal features of the mental illnesses and have an acquaintance with social work. This book has been written with social workers in mind but social work has continuously absorbed knowledge and skills originally developed by others, while others have made use of what was first practised by social workers. The boundaries of many professions have been extended in this mutual exchange and their areas of overlap have grown. I try to keep this diffusion in mind in the hope that some of what I write will also be of interest to other disciplines.

The book has little to say about practice methods, concentrating on what should underlie whatever particular technique is adopted. Little is said about emergency work and the associated legal aspects. The focus is on ongoing work based in the community which is crucially important but which still seems to be provided somewhat reluctantly. Priority has gone to mandatory work: crisis intervention which potentially involves the use of compulsory powers. Investment has also gone into those situations where people can be returned quickly and therefore relatively economically to a productive social role. Long-term work gets what is left–reflecting social values. The National Health Service and Community Care Act 1990 and the shift of policy it represented (Bornat et al., 1997; McDonald, 1999) renewed the debate about provision for people with a mental illness. There was a growing recognition that the lack of facilities in the community was wasteful, leading to constant hospital readmissions, and inhuman in terms of what happened to many people on their discharge from hospital. Prisons, doss-houses and 'cardboard cities' housed a high and growing proportion of mentally-ill people, many of whom had fallen through the net of the mental health services. It has taken a long time, however, for responses to the needs to emerge. The stimulants ultimately, have probably been twofold:

1. the increase in the number of suicides and attempted suicides among young men (including students) (Dept of Health, 1993), and in rural communities (Hawton et al., 1998); and

ix

2. the publicity associated with homicides by mentally ill people
    (Parker and McCulloch, 1999; Zito Trust, 1993).

Within the complex of services needed to respond to the many facets
of the repercussions of mental illness, ongoing longer-term work must
play a crucial part. Without it other aspects of the services will struggle
with inappropriate demands and inappropriate responses. People will
suffer.

The material in this book falls into three parts. Chapters 1–3 examine
what as practitioners we bring into our work: our attitudes to what
constitutes mental health and mental illness and our perceptions of
the psychiatric services. These will profoundly influence what we do
and the decisions we make. Chapters 4–6 consider work with and for
the sufferer, while Chapter 7 looks at work with sufferers' families.
Material put in one place could easily have gone in another: in disen-
tangling an organic situation to trace out its elements and assist our
understanding, what goes where is not always clear-cut but a matter
of choice.

Another problem is language. I have tried to exorcise the 'isms' that
would give offence; but it is very difficult in English not to be sexist,
for example, without resorting to forms of words that make for clumsy
reading. I have tried to get round this occasionally by using a neutral
plural where to be grammatically accurate I should have used the
male and female singular. Other terms also produce difficulties. I have
already used the term 'sufferer' and I will continue to use it since I
have rarely come across anyone with a mental illness who was not
suffering; but it is acknowledged that members of the users' movement
could find the word patronising. It is usual these days to talk of 'carers',
but I find it a bland, overinclusive term. It can cover people with a
financial interest, paid staff, friends, neighbours, sympathetic employers and others who undoubtedly make a valuable contribution to a
sufferer's well-being. The bulk of caring is done by families, though –
in quantity, quality and commitment – and it seems diminishing to
lump them in with a range of others. I will refer to families unless I
mean the whole spectrum of carers. 'Client' is yet another disputed
term which I use in the absence of an agreed alternative.

It is acknowledged from the outset that what has been written
sounds prescriptive, at times smacking of the sort of professionalism
which people might condemn as elitist. I make three points about
this:

1. That social work involving mentally ill people rests upon the same principles as any other kind, not least self-determination;
2. That if we care about our clients we may need to step in to protect them on occasion even from themselves; protection can become a higher priority than self-determination if clients are to survive;
3. That much of what is discussed hereafter a social worker may never be able to implement since it will depend on the cooperation of others, not least the sufferer. That cooperation may be given enthusiastically, grudgingly or not at all. I would still argue it is incumbent on social workers to think through their contribution to improving their clients' situations, to identify the rationale of what they propose and bring this into their discussions with clients, their families, the professional team and the wider network. The social work contribution may be adopted, modified or rejected; but unless it is formulated practitioners are failing their clients, their agency and their profession. I hope that what I write assists this contribution. The alternative – off-the-cuff ad hocery – is not good enough. People deserve better from us.

Throughout I have assumed the social worker is community-based, but more important is the community orientation. Even if the base is a hospital and the primary work with inpatients, it remains crucial to focus on the issues that living in the community raises. Even from a community base it is still possible to have a hospital orientation – reaching for hospital staff and facilities automatically in response to whatever difficulty arises.

The working axioms in Chapters 4–7 are developed for generic application whatever the psychosis involved. My hope in formulating them is that they will prove of practical value, be economic of learning to acquire and underscore the transferability of concepts. Even if the practitioner has little acquaintance with a particular condition s/he will nevertheless have a structure of approach to enable her/him to address the situation with a greater degree of confidence.

It need hardly be added that, where practice examples have been used, names and circumstances have been changed to safeguard confidentiality.

1

Determinants of Practice: Defining Mental Health and Mental Illness

What constitutes mental health

What constitutes mental health is difficult to define. Most attempts at definition (Jahoda, 1958; Maslow, 1969; Vaillant, 1970; McCullogh and Prins, 1978; Hershenson and Power, 1987) appear to group around three elements:

1. *The idea of the mature self* – the sort of people we are. Mentally healthy people will be satisfied with and enjoying their lives. They will have a positive self-image but be realistically aware and accepting of their limitations. Their self-identity will be linked to an underlying philosophy or value system which forms the basis of their integrity and their internalised standards for behaviour. They will have a capacity to learn and develop, factors worthwhile in themselves and necessary if they are to maintain their mental health as their life circumstances change.

2. *Self-management in social relations* – Some literature suggests that our most important capacity is the ability to make and sustain intimate relationships. The number and nature of such relationships may not be specified, but the inference is that close relations with one's parents, one's children and at least one friend are very significant. The epitome of a healthy capacity to relate would appear to be a successful marriage or cohabitation: an ongoing relationship with a member of the opposite sex which includes physical intimacy. Where this leaves stable homosexual relationships is not quite clear.

With this ability to make and sustain intimate relationships is the notion of the ability to retain one's autonomy: the 'one flesh, separate persons' concept of Skynner (1976). Despite the intimacy, the partner is not essential for survival. This idea of autonomy links to another, of being in control of oneself and one's circumstances. A mentally healthy person is not at the mercy of their inner needs, desires or feelings but can control, express and direct them in a socially constructive way. Nor are they at the mercy of other people: they can resist emotional demands, pressures and manipulations without either meekly submitting or angrily rejecting. They can tolerate frustration and postpone gratification as necessary. They can read and respond to social situations with realism and appropriateness; exercise choice and make decisions with objectivity and a greater chance of a successful outcome. Even when engaged in 'non-intimate' relations of the day-to-day kind, they will interact with interest, sensitivity and receptivity to others' messages, conscious of what they are communicating, aware of its effects and modifying matters where this is called for.

3. *The discharge of social roles*, whether these relate to home-based life within family, kinship and neighbourhood groups, to work-related functions, or to recreation/interest activities. To discharge any social role involves a realistic understanding of what general social expectations accrue around that particular role as well as the more particularised ideas of one's immediate social groups. Effective role performance will depend on one's capacity to meet the obligations of that role, together with the ability to adjust that performance, since many roles, such as parent, are developing, not static. Other role performances may have unexpected challenges thrown up within them, from new technology at work to a friend becoming seriously ill, which demand adjustment.

Adjustment is to be distinguished from conformity. Mentally healthy people will be able to choose whether they conform. They have the capacity to evaluate and weigh the social and personal consequences of conforming or not. Most societies and groups will tolerate, in varying degrees, some flexibility in the way roles are executed; but there can be times when individuals are faced with painful, even dangerous choices. To be mentally healthy is not always comfortable, as the records of Amnesty, to name but one organisation, demonstrate.

The discharge of social roles will call for qualities such as a sense of responsibility and a reasonable self-reliance, but will also require the associated technical and social skills. Modern living is making increased demands in technical terms (domestic appliances, computers, cars, form-filling and so on) and in the social sphere (negotiating with bank managers, resisting sales pressures, holidaying abroad, meeting neighbours from different ethnic backgrounds and so on). These represent routine demands: the literature goes on to suggest that the really mentally healthy will also be able to cope with emergencies. They will need problem-solving skills, the ability to handle crises and manage stress, to recognise where to find help when it is needed and a willingness to use it.

Mentally healthy people will make a success of their lives and this will reinforce their competence, self-image and satisfaction. They will have achieved success by approved social processes since means as well as ends are significant. Acquiring wealth is one thing if you earn it, quite another if you steal it.

Criticism and reservations

The literature also contains criticisms and reservations about these definitions of mental health which fall into six groups:

1. There are inherent contradictions in the qualities themselves. For example, it is possible for individuals to be happy with themselves and their lives while being the cause of concern to others by, say, hedonistically sloughing off their social responsibilities.
2. The value of drawing up lists and attributes of mental health has been seriously questioned. To possess all the attributes would be very rare and make their owners, to quote Skynner again (1990) the mental health equivalents of Olympic athletes. Most of us muddle along; not too bad in many respects but not too good in some. Lists represent a preoccupation with idealism which has little to do with the pragmatics of ordinary life.
3. Others have argued that general characteristics do not really exist and that behaviour is specific to situations. There will be times when we respond in a 'mentally healthy' way and others when we do not. Parents will ordinarily respond positively to their children;

but at other times they will ignore them, snap at them, or even strike out at them because at that point parents are tired, worried, absorbed elsewhere or feeling stretched to the limit.

4. Definitions are also accused of being static and focused on adults of working age. Children and elderly people rarely figure. Even within the considered range, the implicit assumption is that people are physically healthy and of average intelligence. What constitutes mental health for the 'others' is largely ignored. The implication, perhaps, is that you cannot expect them to be mentally healthy, which is denigrating to say the least. Definitions also change over time. A mid-Victorian list of attributes would be very different from a modern one, especially in respect of women. Whether there are, or should be, differences in attributes based on sex is a point seldom raised. Some research suggests there could be innate differences between the sexes, which suggests there should be different criteria for mental healthiness. Others would argue that different expectations of men and women are rooted in socially determined gender roles and reflect another facet of discrimination.

5. Definitions suggest that mentally healthy people can cope with anything life throws at them. I doubt this, and much prefer Bartlett's (1970) approach, which looks at the balance between coping resources and the demands being made upon them. People can break down if either their resources leave them unable to cope with 'normal' demands, or the demands are so excessive that even the most resourceful would collapse under the pressure. 'Not coping' is not *a priori* a reflection of an intrinsic lack of mental health. The social and physical environment in which we live has a profound significance. Many studies have demonstrated that poverty, illness, poor housing, poor education, unemployment and social isolation can 'seriously damage your [mental] health' (Pilgrim and Rogers, 1999). To distinguish between these two broad categories of explanation of breakdown – inadequate resources or excessive demands – or to establish the degree of balance between them in a specific situation – is crucial in practice. Goals and means used in social work intervention will be very different for each.

6. The final criticism is perhaps the most profound. Endemic to any definition is a value system, expressed as a set of ideals or a notion of preferences. Derived from these are concepts of what consti-

tutes normal behaviour and what is appropriate to the various social roles. As individuals with variations we are nevertheless largely the products of a socialisation process geared to producing a current and future society with a sufficient cohesion to survive.

Mental health definitions, then, are typically specific to a particular culture and may have little relevance for any other. The definitions summarised above, for example, are overwhelmingly drawn from Western democratic societies – inevitably. They were the most accessible and the most meaningful to me given my own cultural background and their relevance to my work, since the bulk of my clients and colleagues shared that cultural heritage. Herein lies the danger. This cultural selectivity can reinforce my attitudes, add to my conviction that I am 'right', that my views are the 'normal' ones and that 'everyone' shares them. I adopt them for practice with little questioning. This acculturation process always risked practice outcomes in a predominantly class-oriented society; it would be fatal to good practice in a multicultural one (Banks, 1999; Bhugra and Bahl, 1999)

Influence on practice

We all need to examine our ideas of what constitutes mental health, since they are going to profoundly colour our perceptions of what is 'wrong' in the situations we deal with and how, ideally, we would like things to be: that is our assessment and goals. We even use them in our choice of methods. If we believe getting problems out into the open and discussing them is the mature way to handle difficulties, then we are probably going to opt for one of the 'talking cures'; not just for itself but also as an exemplar to clients for dealing with any problems in the future. If mentally healthy people are self-directing, behavioural modification methods can be seen as manipulative and therefore may be eschewed. If maturity is a matter of saying outright what you think and feel, Rogerian approaches would seem to be more appropriate. If you believe people are innately capable but the social systems they live in are crippling this capacity, then the way to assist would be to work with them in groups to empower them and get systems changed.

There is the endemic risk that practitioners' ideas of mental healthiness will open up gaps between them and the people they are trying to help. For example, social work has been criticised in the past for seeking to change people by lengthy, quasi-analytic 'deep' casework. Problems were deemed personal, individual and probably connected to childhood experiences. Counselling, therefore, was what people were offered, whether or not it was what they wanted or needed. We now have sense enough to realise that as a method it has relevance to a narrower range of problems and clients: those who can use mainly verbal means to tackle moderately severe emotional problems.

Research by Sainsbury, Nixon and Phillips (1982) suggested there was still a considerable gulf between social workers' and clients' perceptions of problems. Social workers tended to see more difficulties than clients and to focus on emotion/relationship issues. Clients tended to see fewer problems and regard them as basically practical. Which perception is 'correct' becomes almost irrelevant: worker and client are operating at cross-purposes. Clients became increasingly disillusioned with their workers, and workers dispirited by what they saw as their clients' failure to make 'progress'. Whether these value discrepancies reflected workers' professional preferences or a different socialisation is a matter of debate; the misfit with clients' constructs remained.

If gaps of this sort are probably sub-cultural, other gaps may be cultural. Feminists, for example, would argue that we live in a world shaped to suit men, with institutionalised sexism. Psychiatric services, among others, remain male-dominated despite the (reducing) majority of users being women. Women have had to fight for recognition of their particular problems (Barnes and Maple, 1992; Abel *et al.*, 1996) and have resorted to developing their own projects and services out of dissatisfaction with conventional provision. To rather turn the argument on its head in the light of the increase in suicides/ attempted suicides among younger men, the question is raised as to whether the organisation of psychiatric services are inappropriate for them too. Unwitting collusion with institutionalised oppression is a constant risk. Sheppard (1991) suggests, in examining referrals for compulsory admission under the Mental Health Act, these were a means for the social control of women.

With so many possible gaps within a culture, the potential gaps when working across cultures are even wider. As practitioners in a multiracial, multiethnic society we need to acknowledge that our own cultural identity can be seen as a threat by people from other backgrounds, and we may feel threatened by them in addition to any other potential source of gap such as (crucially) differences in language and all the complications of the use of interpreters. We need to consciously learn about other cultures if they are not part of our experience. In particular, we will need to understand how problems are defined, the causations which are assigned to them and the culturally approved means of dealing with them – in other words, to understand how mental healthiness is interpreted in those cultures. If we fail to understand, our work is going to be justifiably criticised as racially and/or ethnically prejudiced (Rack, 1982; Littlewood and Lipsedge, 1997; Fernando, 1995; Jenkinson, 1988; Palmer, 1999; Bhugra and Bahl, 1999; Banks, 1999). The overrepresentation of black people detained by the criminal justice system or subjected to the use of compulsion under the Mental Health Act should give us pause. We need to look hard to see if the reason lies in our biases. They may be a matter of sheer ignorance or real prejudice: both can and need to be remedied once they have been identified.

Social work practice utilises ordinary socio-emotional processes; the difference lies in recognising, selecting and employing those processes which foster our professional objectives – to try to resolve people's difficulties in social functioning which come within our sphere of competence and the remit of our employing agencies. Only when we recognise what is at work within ourselves and our own socio-emotional functioning will we be able to identify whether we are really matching needs objectively and, if not, amending what we are doing to close the gaps generated by culture, subculture, socialisation or our personal 'hang-ups'. For social workers self-awareness is an essential, not a luxury (Bryant, 2000). To develop that awareness is likely to be painful, calling for a good deal of mental healthiness in ourselves.

What constitutes mental illness

If we are uncertain about what constitutes mental health, there is no more clarity about what constitutes mental illness. It is possible to think of mental health and mental illness as a continuum: the Olympians at one end and the insane at the other, with most of us scattered somewhere around the middle. I am not convinced of the usefulness of this notion. While the Olympians would be regarded as exceptional, they would not be seen as 'abnormal', as mentally ill people typically are. There is a disjuncture somewhere along the line and the qualitative distinction would appear to be grounded in whether people can be held responsible for their actions or not. The problem is how to establish this.

In Britain, the law, for example, is very concerned about this issue of responsibility. It is a defence to plead insanity (in effect, 'I was not responsible for my actions'), though this plea will be tested in court (Prins, 1995). Responsible people are subject to the rigour of the law for illegal behaviour: 'not responsible' people can be 'sentenced' to treatment. Diminished responsibility is a halfway-house plea which may end in punishment, but punishment that is less severe than it would otherwise have been. This dilemma, whether to punish or to treat, runs like a thread through many of our dealings with offenders and reflects society's uncertainty in some cases about culpability. Arguably, the probation service was originally called into existence to assist the legal system to handle this dilemma by offering help, even if it was by means of a 'sentence' through a probation order. The dilemmas have always been particularly acute in dealing with juvenile offenders: patently in determining the age of criminal responsibility and distinguishing between children, young persons and adults. Even if they have technically been found guilty of crime, policy over the years has swung between dealing with children and young persons on the 'treatment' model, based on the idea that offending was one expression of socio-emotional deprivation, and the 'justice' model, which focused on the offence, not the social background. In the 1950s and 1960s, the 'deprived' (treatment) view of delinquency predominated. In more recent times the 'depraved' (control) view seems to hold the greater sway as social tolerance of juvenile crime has eroded. For the treatment lobby this has raised dilemmas. Two constant criticisms have been made: the effectiveness of treatment methods have been questioned, while the indefinite duration and lack of discharge criteria for them have been regarded as incompatible with notions of social justice. Similar offences should merit a similar 'sentence' of predetermined length. Not that 'control' methods have had much better success if post-custodial relapse rates are any guide.

A further dilemma has now emerged: whether treatment is possible in certain cases or not – at least where some adults are concerned. Some psychiatrists are arguing that, as a mental illness, severe personality disorder is untreatable and that as a consequence the 'criminal' provisions of the Mental Health Act cannot be used to detain 'dangerous' people. They have to be processed through the ordinary criminal justice system as though they were responsible for their actions. This leaves them to the vagaries of the prison psychiatric services, but more significantly it means that once their sentence has been completed they are discharged into the community whether considered still dangerous or not. The 'safeguard' of detention for treatment, that people will not be discharged until considered safe, cannot be applied. How to plug this gap in the supervision of people seen as a potential danger to the public has given rise to proposals (Dept of Health, 2000) that they could be detained compulsorily to a specialised service whether or not they have committed a crime. Moreover, as in the case of sex offenders, the appropriate public services would be notified when a detainee was returned into the community. To balance public protection against civil liberties (especially the provisions of the Human Rights Act) is a delicate matter not easily resolved; and these suggestions will be a source of contention.

However, nobody would suggest that all misbehaviours could be attributed to a mental illness, especially if not just legal offences are included but all the objectionable, upsetting or out-of-the-ordinary behaviours we encounter from time to time in daily living. Apart from any differences we might have about what to include as 'misbehaviour', we would ordinarily have a variety of explanations about what lay behind it. After the rioting in Newcastle-upon-Tyne in 1991, for example, the explanations offered included poverty, social alienation, unemployment, hopelessness due to the lack of future prospects, the paucity of clubs and centres, poor housing, poor education, the lack of good parenting, the moral degeneration of society, Thatcherite materialism, organised criminality and downright evil. The judgments we make will be coloured by our general ideas about 'people', personal experiences which seem to us to have some relevance, what we know (or think we know) about this situation and what engages our particular sympathies or revulsions. As a truism, what we can understand adds to our tolerance; what we find incomprehensible adds to our impatience. It is a complex process by which we begin to formulate our ideas about the forces at work, who or what is responsible, where any fault or blame lies and consequently what ought to be done, by whom, to put matters 'right'. The more people involved in the discussion, the more diversity of view is likely.

Approaches to defining mental illness

If we do not ascribe all 'misbehaviours' to mental illness, we are still left to decide what we do include and what we attribute elsewhere. It seems to me there are basically three possible stances we can adopt:

1. *The widest stance* regards as mental health problems all break-downs in coping and the associated pain. MIND (the National Association for Mental Health in the UK) uses the term 'mental distress' to define the focus of its concern, but no boundaries are put around the causation of that distress. Neuroses, psychoses, breakdowns in relationships, bereavement, discrimination, victimisation, helplessness, lack of services, oppressive economic, political or social systems could be just some of the potential distress-creating factors.

   Though the range is still wide, Hershenson and Power (1987), for example, limit what they consider mental ill-health to four broad areas of problem: (a) social behaviour (disabilities in social skills, making relationships, handling aggression and coping with social expectations); (b) emotional behaviour (where problems give rise to depression, anxiety, phobias and so on); (c) health-related issues (a diverse group including insomnia, pain control and destructive behaviours from smoking to drug abuse); and (d) work-related issues (another extensive group ranging from boredom to burnout; from unemployment to 'workaholicism'). Their approach seems to have more in common with the psycho-social approach familiar to social work students who have read their Hollis (1972) and Perlman (1957).

   What this widest definition seems to involve, in effect, is the problems of human living, but the sufferers are so diverse it is impossible to see them accepting a common 'I am mentally ill' identity. Even on a psychiatric hospital ward I have heard those patients suffering basically from neurotic conditions assert, 'I am not like them' – the sufferers from psychotic conditions. The variety of causations would require a variety of remedial meth-ods and a range of organisational frameworks to implement them. Partialisation would be the only way forward, with interested groups cohering around specific issues – such as the Mental Health Alliance responding to proposed changes to mental health legis-lation. It is doubtful whether the component elements would cohere as a mental health movement, particularly given the stigma still associated with mental illness. The temptation to identify elsewhere would be strong: elements would see their problems as associated with such matters as politics, education or medicine – the more powerful and acceptable social institutions. People could share a common humanity and a common concern for a particular form of suffering – mental distress – but that would be as far as it went. This leaves a place for organisations such as MIND to identify issues, publicise, lobby, advocate and bring together those involved (whether service providers or service consumers; problem 'creators' or 'victims'), but I cannot see mental health ever becoming a popular mass movement. To take on a sea of troubles, call them mental health problems and expect a cohesive response is unrealistic.

2. *A more limited view* of the boundaries of mental ill-health is what we expect of psychiatry. The logic here is that, since psychiatrists are deemed to be the experts in mental disorders, what (Western) society expects them to take care of would be a reasonable guide to what society generally includes in its definition. One of the disorders psychiatry has been expected to deal with is mental impairment. I think this has helped to compound confusion in the public mind between impairment and mental illness. Even the quality media get the distinction wrong from time to time. Fortunately we are in the process of redefining impairment as a socio-educational matter rather than a medical one, so there is reason to hope this confusion will gradually clear. The process would be speeded if impairment was dealt with under separate legislation, as it was for many years after 1913, instead of being pushed in with the Mental Health Acts. For the purposes of this argument I am excluding mental impairment, except insofar as impaired people can also suffer from a mental illness.

   In terms of mental illness, it seems that psychiatrists are expected to contribute in the following situations:

   (a) Emotional disorders. While these may be of any kind and patients of any age, two areas in particular have been developed: (i) child and family guidance; and (ii) the treatment of certain syndromes which are generally regarded as emotionally-based and collectively identified as the neuroses, including acute and chronic anxiety states, eating disorders, phobias, obsessional compulsive disorders, hysteria and some sexual dysfunctions. I also think of reactive depression as an emotional disorder, different from endogenous depression which I regard as a psychosis.

(b) Disorders which are associated with emotional disturbance such as drug addiction and alcoholism, attempted suicide, sexual deviations and psychosomatic conditions.

(c) Aspects of social malfunctioning which also have connotations of emotional disorder in the sense that they are ascribed to a disorder of personality. The clear extreme here is the so-called psychopathic personality, but the range of disorder is wide, from dangerous criminality to people who seem to have blind spots – areas of self-management which experience does not change and which produce recurring social difficulties.

(d) The psychoses, by which is meant schizophrenia (or the schizophrenias and including paraphrenia), the affective psychoses (endogenous depression, mania and manic depressive psychosis) and the dementias.

I am not convinced that the first three groups are illnesses in the usually accepted sense of that word. I sympathise with Eysenck's argument (1975) that disorders of function of this kind are not fundamentally medical matters. They became so perhaps by association (and in the process became 'illnesses') because of the pioneering work undertaken by doctors – Freud being the obvious example – at a time when there were no other recognised professions to whom treatment could be entrusted. Psychology and social work, for example, were recognised much later. Medicine's involvement with these disorders suited society. To be able to label some 'deviances' illnesses and hand them over to doctors to deal with has the semblance of being humane as well as solving the problem of finding other ways to deal with them. The notion that unhappy people are sick people goes back at least as far as Samuel Butler's *Erewhon*.

Ivan Illich's warnings (1977) of the dangers of encroaching medicalisation (still persisting in the view of Kutchins and Kirk, 1999) and the power it puts into the hands of a profession notoriously hard to bring to account are not to be ignored; but these conditions create much human misery and it is fortunate that there are trained doctors around to give their help. What I am arguing, though, is that medicine now has no monopoly for work in this sphere, but shares it with psychology and social work. It has devolved still further as other professional groups have made use of what has been developed: counsellors, psychiatric nurses, occupational therapists, teachers (especially those in pastoral care posts), youth workers and many others share concerns and methods. This is a healthy development. It means that numerically there are more skilled people around (if still not enough), and there are far more channels by which people may gain access to a service. Psychiatry still suffers from the stigma of association with 'madness' and for this reason many people strongly resist a referral. With more socially acceptable access points there is more chance of getting at problems early, with a better chance of success.

3. *The narrowest view* (if we accept the argument that emotional and personality disorders are not the exclusive concern of medicine and are therefore at the least doubtfully illnesses) is that the only certain mental illnesses are the psychoses. The justifications for this are possibly twofold. First, even according to the psychiatry textbooks, the psychoses are qualitatively different. People suffering from the neuroses may see realities in a distorted way and react accordingly, but they are in touch with those realities. People suffering from a psychosis, in varying degrees and over a varying range of aspects of their lives, have lost contact with part, sometimes most, of that reality and are responding to an inner generated perception. This qualitative difference is not related to the severity of the condition, since for some people their neurosis is agonisingly, totally life-disrupting, while some with a psychosis experience but little pain or social disruption. The qualitative difference remains, however.

Second, this qualitative difference seems to carry over into people's perceptions. Neuroses and personality disorders are seen as exaggerations of feelings and behaviour but still connected to ordinary human experience. Psychotics are seen as in another world. The normal expectations do not apply and we are very uncertain how to deal with them. This perception of psychosis is a very mixed blessing. On the one hand uncertainty leaves us vulnerable to fears and fantasies about 'madness' – violence in particular – and these can be reinforced by media exploitation. People with psychosis are consequently misunderstood, isolated

and stigmatised, together with their families. There are pressures around for 'something to be done': if they cannot be cured
quickly, then remove them before 'something happens' – the
origin of the 'not in my backyard' attitude (Dunn, 1999) which
can sometimes make rehabilitation programmes so difficult to
implement. On the other hand, if people with a mental illness
are seen as not being responsible for their actions, there is the
possibility that merely odd behaviour will be tolerated or indulged
without the customary social sanctions being applied. It becomes
possible for some people to retain a place in society which otherwise they might not have done.

Even if we accept that the psychoses are the true mental illnesses,
we will still get disputes in borderline cases as to whether a particular
individual is ill or not. In court, for example, defence and prosecution
will call expert witnesses to support diametrically opposed points of
view about the culpability of the accused. Moreover, even if it is
agreed that people are suffering from a psychosis, there is no unanimity of view about the cause of it. I return to this in the next chapter.

Influence on practice

Just as our attitudes to mental health will affect our perceptions of
the nature of the difficulties, our goals and the means of attaining them,
so will our views of mental illness. If we adopt parameter 1 above
we have an enormously wide choice of what we address, from what
operational base, by what method and involving a selection of
professional or occupational 'hats'. For instance, if I felt that unemployment was a primary determinant of mental illness, I could tackle
it by getting involved in individual counselling, mutual support groups,
groups which sought to develop interests and hobbies as alternative
sources of satisfaction and esteem; through welfare rights work; through
public or sponsored employment training schemes such as the
Welfare to Work programme; by assisting the setting up of worker
co-operatives or by becoming an employer myself. If one of the
explanations of unemployment was the powerful position of employers over employees, a logical choice would be involvement with the
trade union movement. I could campaign to get the government to
do something about it, or I might, through the media, try to work

up pressure on the issue. I could take up politics to get elected to a position of influence, or I might feel that nothing would be achieved by parliamentary change: unemployment is inevitable under a capitalist system and the only real answer is direct action. All these activities are arguably relevant if the range of systems involved in the issue, from the individual to the societal, are to be tackled by appropriate means. For me, this might amount to a social welfare movement, but to suggest that all 'dis-welfares' such as unemployment result in mental illness is unreasonable – as the great majority of the victims of 'dis-welfare' would agree, I am sure. Distressed, yes; mentally ill, certainly not.

We will be looking at the second parameter, psychiatry, in some detail in the next chapter, but there are points which should be made here. The primary social responsibility of psychiatry is to treat individuals. In that sense its scope and methodology are much more circumscribed than those inferred in parameter 1. Nevertheless psychiatrists see a wide range of problems reflecting most of the 'public issues' confronting society as well as the 'private sorrows'. What will bring people the way of a psychiatrist is not so much the problem as the symptoms or syndrome they are displaying as a result.

The diversity of symptomatologies with their wider range of origins has pushed psychiatry in different ways – three in particular:

(1) Into specialisation. Even the three main fields (mental impairment, adult psychiatry and child and family guidance) have subdivided further into such areas as psychogeriatrics, addictions, forensics, adolescent psychiatry; and into specialisation by method, from relaxation to confrontation, from individual psychoanalysis to family and group therapy;

(2) Into disagreement. The range of possible problems behind what appear to be a similar group of symptoms has led to considerable divergences of view about causation, and consequently what is the appropriate means of treatment. Again, we will be looking at this in more detail in the next chapter.

(3) Despite differences, psychiatry (like other professional groups) has individually and collectively spoken out on issues of public policy that have emerged in their professional practice.

Social workers who use this parameter of approach to defining mental illness cannot avoid similar issues. They will have to decide on their specialism and examine explanations of causation; and where they stand on professional issues, not just to establish a basis for their own work but to provide a foundation for orientation to the clinical team, since clinical team-work is a crucial characteristic of parameters 2 and 3. Teams have to work out a sufficient unanimity of approach if they are not to reduce themselves, patients, families and others to confusion. Though more comprehensible than parameter 1 (distress), parameter 2 (psychiatry) is still very wide in its scope, remains hazy and ambiguous in various respects and has internal contradictions. It therefore remains an unsatisfactory basis for defining what we mean by mental illness. My own choice is parameter 3, the psychoses only, and I have five reasons to support this:

(1)   There is very little dispute that these are mental illnesses, so the boundaries of concern are relatively specific and clear.
(2)   To distinguish them in this way seems to reflect both the clinical and popular conceptions.
(3)   It takes emotional and personality disorders clear of the stigma which persists around mental illness. At the same time, with only the psychoses to focus upon, it might well be easier to foster public understanding (as we have begun to do with Alzheimer's disease) and reduce the stigma anyway.
(4)   The qualitative distinctions in the conditions suggest that qualitative distinctions are required in practice in response. We need to clarify what these are if we are to offer the best service.
(5)   A recognition of its particular nature might raise the status of work with psychotically ill people. Work with people with neuroses currently seems to have pride of place. Need insists that sufferers from psychosis have parity.

It is this stance towards defining mental illness that is adopted for the purposes of this book.

2

Determinants of Practice: Attitudes to Psychiatry

Attitudes to psychiatry change over time (Shorter, 1997), often reflect our ambivalent feelings about it, and are complicated by the conflicts within psychiatry itself. There are three areas of confusion to address if our approach to psychiatry is to provide a rational footing for our work: our expectations of psychiatrists, social attitudes to psychiatric practice and the disagreements within psychiatry about the origins of psychosis.

Expectations of psychiatrists

There is a popular misconception that psychiatrists are psychoanalysts. The association owes much to historical accident, in that Freud was a doctor and psychoanalysis became, *de facto* if not *de jure*, a matter for the medical profession. The analytic mystique has been both developed and distorted by many films and television series. The infallible psychiatrist penetratingly sees what lies behind behaviour; once he has established this and revealed all (typically some earlier trauma), everything is cured and people live happily ever after. This scenario has little to do with medicine, psychiatry or psychoanalysis: it has much more to do with wish fulfilment. We are all susceptible to it, professionals included. The reality of psychiatric practice at times has been almost buried under what we have projected onto it, to the intense discomfort of psychiatrists.

False expectations

In my practice I was involved with people suffering from neuroses and psychoses, but much of my work was with people who suffered from neither in the textbook sense. They were people with social problems or who were regarded as social problems by others. They were fundamentally no different from people figuring in the caseloads of social workers in almost any other setting. That they had come the way of psychiatry was almost fortuitous. In retrospect, there seem to be three main reasons for this. First, under pressure they had made a suicidal gesture, or had threatened one, and had been referred to a psychiatrist on the grounds that they were suffering from depression. At worst they were experiencing a transient depression – a matter of mood lasting from a few hours to a few days and invariably reactive. They could just as well have expressed their distress, however occasioned, by getting drunk, hitting someone, going shoplifting or turning up at a casualty department complaining of severe stomach pain. These alternative expressions would have landed them in different arenas with different outcomes. This is one illustration of the symptoms rather than the problems determining what is deemed a mental health matter and a psychiatrist's concern.

Second, people had complained, perhaps to their social worker or GP, that they were utterly miserable. Given their circumstances or the circumstances in which they had landed themselves, their feelings of despair were understandable; but they were again seized upon as evidence of a depressive illness and the complainant was referred to a psychiatrist. This sort of referral was sometimes born of a sense of helplessness in the referrer: caught between not knowing how to help but feeling they had to do something. A referral was at least an appearance of action and a way out of their dilemma.

Third, a referral was made out of sheer frustration and its concomitant, irritation. The person-with-a-problem had been back time and again; nothing that had been tried by way of problem-solving had worked. Promising starts, like the seeds that fell by the wayside, had quickly withered, producing no material change. So they were sent on to the underlying-problem finders, people changers and cure-alls – psychiatrists. Among others, courts can feel like this about petty offenders. With all the potential disposals exhausted, they remand for psychiatric reports.

The referrers' feelings may be understandable, but they have really misunderstood what psychiatry can offer in such circumstances. It may be able to say what behaviour is *not* due to, and may offer an *opinion* as to what it might be attributable. The report would probably add a rather gloomy prognosis, little in the way of advice and rarely include any offer of treatment. I can recall colleagues in other agencies complaining vociferously that all they got back from psychiatrists was largely a restatement of the material in their original referral report, together with a 'You carry on because there is nothing I can do that you cannot.' I think the psychiatrists were right: in such situations social work has more to offer than psychiatry. Moreover, for little return, the person referred now had the additional stigma of a psychiatric history which could be used to his/her disadvantage by prospective employers, insurance companies, neighbours, family and social workers – a factor any referrer should bear in mind when weighing up the advantages and disadvantages of a referral in the first place.

If all this sounds harsh on referrers let me also acknowledge from experience the many difficult mental illness situations which were supported and contained by general practitioners, health visitors, district nurses, social workers from other agencies and many others. I was sometimes very glad I was only being used as a consultant rather than taking the responsibility for some very trying work they were doing well.

Appropriate expectations

If there are times when we bring psychiatry in where we should not, there are times when we may not but should. Here I would like to qualify what was said in the previous chapter – that emotional disorders and disturbances of personality were areas of practice shared with other disciplines. This is ordinarily true, but there is a particular contribution medicine generally and psychiatry especially can make. There are three aspects to this:

1. *To establish whether or not there is an organic basis for the disturbances in behaviour.* A good many physical conditions first manifest themselves by changes in feelings and behaviour. Thyroid dysfunction is just one from a potential catalogue. It is too easy, sometimes, to ascribe symptoms to 'mental' causes – more especially where the sufferer already has a bit of a reputation. In practice I heard a range of 'horror stories' such as the woman who was diagnosed as an hysteric when she was actually displaying the initial symptoms of multiple sclerosis; and the man treated as a depressive until it eventually became apparent he had a brain tumour. This is not meant to be critical of doctors: diagnosis is a difficult art.

It is equally important for doctors to recognise where there are socio-emotional problems which are presented to them as physical complaints. There is the well-documented phenomenon of a much higher reported incidence of physical complaints by the recently bereaved, for example. Just as a brain tumour will not be cured by Tofranil, aspirin does little to ease the pain of grief. There are also a range of conditions which initially look like psychoses but are not. People high on drugs can hallucinate and an elderly person can present as confused when they have a high temperature due to an infection. In all such circumstances a differential diagnosis is crucially important if people are to get the appropriate treatment.

Social work tends to see behaviour in psychological or sociological terms. Experience of working as part of a clinical team taught me to respect the physical dimension, too. It is this comprehensiveness in approach to behavioural phenomena that, in my view, justifies rooting psychiatry in medicine rather than elsewhere. Social work should respect what medicine can offer and, whenever a physical factor may be an element, refer-on to establish whether it is or not.

2. *There may be a case for the selective, short-term use of psychotropic drugs*, to help bring acute symptoms under control, to enable some restoration of social functioning, and to give other means of help (such as counselling) the time they need to bring about change. For this we will need a doctor to assess and prescribe. This is an area in which we now know that a great deal of caution is needed: it is easy to create an emotional or physical dependency on, say, tranquillisers and make rather than solve problems. I return to this later.

3. *We will need medical help where physical factors become involved*: patently in the case of attempted suicide or other life-threatening conditions such as anorexia. Compulsive washing can leave hands almost skinless; in psychosomatic conditions the treatment of the 'soma' will still need to be managed while psychotherapy, say, is tackling the 'psyche'.

Psychiatry and psychosis

It was said above that the psychoses are the particular responsibility of psychiatry; this is where psychiatric medicine is at its best in my view and at its most crucial for both diagnosis and treatment. In our present state of knowledge drug treatments are the primary means we have to bring acute psychotic symptoms under control, and the maintenance of medication remains a key factor in preventing relapse. We need to know about drugs since most of our clients will be on medication of one sort or another (Tyrer, Harrison-Read and Van Horn, 1997). Drug treatments on their own are clearly not enough: rehabilitation and dealing with the socio-emotional factors which contributed to the illness, or which the illness has created, will call upon a wide range of skills and disciplines. Medicine, however, remains the lynchpin for now, with its power to prescribe.

Many people – professionals, carers and above all, users – are rightly suspicious of drug use, especially when they are given little explanation of what the drugs are for, how they work, what effects and side-effects they may have, how long they may be needed with what risks, and what, if any, alternative treatments might be available to enable a sufferer to make an informed decision (Lacey, 1996; Breggin, 1993). Drugs can be prescribed for dubious reasons such as the control of behaviour, not in the interest of the sufferer but for the benefit of others, to make the sufferer easier for them to manage whether on the ward, at the day centre or at home. Concerns about the use of Ritalin to alter the behaviours of difficult young children is but one example. Reaching for prescriptions and pills can be seen as the easier way out. This tendency can be buttressed by the idea that physical responses (tablets) for a physical problem (an organic malfunction) is more personally and socially acceptable than a painful look at what we are contributing to problematic interactions. On the other hand we are rightly angry when people get pushed into using drugs simply because they do not have the resources they need (whether sufficient ward staff or enough time during surgery hours) and there is no practical alternative. These are abuses rather than uses of drugs. Moreover, they stigmatise all drug use, making the proper use of them that much more difficult.

Decisions on medication may not be entirely within the control of the sufferer in the sense that s/he can only really choose from which is available and offered. (and doctors do have their preferences). What is on offer may not be entirely within the control the doctor either (Rayner, 2001) The old (typical) anti-psychotic drugs can have distressing side effects; new (atypical) drugs produce far fewer. The new drugs are much more costly and not available in all health districts currently – the 'post-code' hazard that the National Institute of Clinical Excellence is there to address. A particular worry is that people who give up their medication because of the side effects might be coerced into receiving it again under the proposed provisions for compulsory treatment in the community. It would probably be the typical drugs that would be used in any compulsion as only these are available in depot form as yet.

In my practice I have also appreciated the psychiatrist as consultant. Although I have been involved with many people suffering from a psychosis, there were times when it was not always easy to say which. The medical diagnosis might have been schizophrenia, but such were the mood swings the sufferer presented more of a manic depressive picture at times. Or an elderly person suffering from depression would come across as confused occasionally. It was very helpful to talk through the vicissitudes in the course of the illness with someone knowledgeable.

This has been particularly true when dealing with depression. The texts typically make a distinction between neurotic/reactive and endogenous/psychotic depression, and for the most part I have found this distinction valid and important. In reactive depression a socio-emotional perspective was needed: the origins lay in anything from grinding poverty to bereavement. Any medication was an adjunct to the main thrust of remedical action, whether getting hold of practical resources or counselling. For psychotic depressions, medication (anti-depressants or, as a last resort, electro-convulsive therapy) had to form the basis with other methods used supplementarily. Just as drugs are no more than a palliative in a reactive depression, talking cures make little impact on a psychotic depression. At times, though, the distinction between the types of depression was far from easy to make. Sometimes people appeared to slide from the reactive to the psychotic. As the way we feel can affect the way we function physically, maybe what started out as one became the other. It is also possible the underlying psychotic depression was missed originally in the way people presented. Sufferers from an endogenous depression very often try to find an explanation for the way they feel and can quite realistically sometimes offer a rationale indicative of a reactive depression. Again discussing how to handle matters (even if it was only possible in the end to say, 'Keep your options open') was valuable.

Readers may or may not share my perceptions and experience of psychiatry, but it will be obvious how they have influenced my approach. Whatever their views, social workers in mental health need to think through their own expectations since their work will be similarly coloured by them. We will be under pressure not just from others but from within ourselves to keep psychiatry out or to get it in. We may be disillusioned about psychiatrists, dislike drug treatments, or want to protect clients from stigma and therefore avoid referring. Conversely, we may suffer from over-expectations, helplessness and frustration, want the comfort of a second confirming opinion, or to hand over leadership to a more powerful figure who will take responsibility and tell us what to do; so we will want to refer. Prejudice either way is unlikely to serve a client's best interests.

Social attitudes to psychiatric practice

As practitioners we cannot avoid the impact of social attitudes regarding psychiatric practice. Our own attitudes are likely to have been influenced by them and we will undoubtedly run up against them among the people we encounter in the course of our work. Looking back, the high point of public trust of psychiatry was reached in the late 1950s, epitomised by the 1959 Mental Health Act. This sought to put the treatment of mental illness on the same footing as that of physical illness as far as possible. Where compulsion remained, this was taken out of the judicial process and very largely given to the professionals. This was also the era of pharmacological breakthroughs in the treatment of mental illness which made it seem all the more appropriate to put matters into medical hands The climate has changed since, in response to a three-pronged attack: from anti-psychiatry, anti-institutionalism and civil liberties.

Anti-psychiatry

The anti-psychiatry movement (discussed in Clare, 1976; Johnstone, 1988) challenged the very basis of traditional, medically oriented psychiatry. From a psychoanalytic, existentialist or a humanist perspective, people criticised what they regarded as an authoritarian, hospital-dominated, drug-prescribing regimen. They called for ways of working which put respect for the sufferer at the centre of concern, followed his or her needs and met them in individualised ways, free from coercive professionalism, indiscriminate medication and rigid organisational systems. The anti-psychiatry movement seems to have ebbed in recent years but to have handed on its particular torch to the user movement, appropriately enough. This movement argues for the recognition of the consumer's right to be the principal determinant of his/her treatment at the individual level, and consumers collectively the principal determinants of the forms of service at the level of provision. The professional's 'I know what is best for you' is an unacceptable abuse of power (Cohen, 1990).

Anti-institutionalism

The second thrust has come from anti-institutionalism. In the 1940s, 1950s and 1960s a spate of research literature was published criticising children's homes, homes for elderly people, prisons and mental hospitals (Curtis, 1946; Townsend, 1962; Morris, 1963; Goffman, 1968). Inmates were dehumanised and processed through systems set up for the convenience of the staff, not the needs of the residents. Utterly dependent, hidden from public view, inmates could be victimised and had little chance to protest except in minor individual ways. On discharge people were more disabled than before: deskilled by 'batch' living, they were severely handicapped in doing things or making decisions for themselves (Barton, 1959). Elaborate rehabilitation schemes became necessary to return people to the community. It is arguable that the pressure for care in the community is more a result of anti-institutionalism than any positive idea of what community care comprises, since the term seems to mean very different things to different people (Goodwin, 1990).

Anti-institutionalism received a boost from the normalisation movement (CMH, 1981). Philosophically the movement is concerned with inequality of citizenship and the stigmatising effect that specialised provision, including institutions, has upon disadvantaged groups, reinforcing their status as second-class, sub-citizens. Rather than creating specialised discriminatory services, the movement advocates the use of the normal, socially acceptable, integrative routes that would not separate people – inclusive provision, not exclusive. If the needs were educational, these should not be met in special schools and training centres but in mainstream schools and further education colleges.

It was on the back of these concerns that the programme of closing the huge Victorian mental hospitals was largely based. Few would regret their passing. More would regret that the resources they consumed and the range of functions that they served were not adequately transferred to alternative community-based services.

Civil liberties

The third line of attack came from the civil liberties lobby, led by Larry Gostin (1975) of MIND. Professionals were abusing their power, and the rights of individuals were being overridden. The injustices were such that new legislation was the only way to establish adequate systems to safeguard those rights. The subsequent 1983 Mental Health Act curtailed the powers of the professionals to detain and treat, while strengthening the powers of patients to appeal to legal process. It is proposed (Dept of Health, 2000) that this process be carried further in that independent mental health tribunals, after a full hearing (including expert witnesses and patients' advocates), would decide whether people should be detained for longer periods of six to twelve months – in contrast to the present position in which tribunals act as a kind of appeal court against decisions taken by professionals.

More recently (Pedler, 1999), while still concerned with legal process, a more rights-oriented approach has been developed and promoted by the Mental Health Alliance aimed at extending user self-determination. The rights sought include a right to an individual assessment of needs for all patients not just those subject to compulsion, and a duty to provide the required treatment; the right to determine their own treatment as long as they have the capacity (though in itself capacity remains a thorny issue – Dawson and McDonald, 2000), but also to make binding advance directives should they become incapacitated together with rights to protection should the incapacity be prolonged as with, say, advanced dementia. Users' experiences of psychiatric services are the evidence base for the changes sought (Rogers, Pilgrim and Lacey, 1993; Barker, Campbell and Davidson, 1999).

Influence on practice

Again, we need to think through where we stand on these issues. To oversimplify to the point of absurdity, an extreme anti-psychiatry stance would imply that in no way would I become involved with or condone my client getting involved with any aspect of traditional psychiatry; it is so damaging that I would always seek alternatives. As an anti-institutionalist extremist, I might be prepared to use some psychiatric services but I would never countenance an admission to hospital or any other sort of residential establishment since these, too, are so damaging. As a civil liberties protagonist I could feel so strongly that in no circumstance would I be prepared to use compulsion; it would always be the greater of two evils and I would try to persuade others (such as the nearest relative) not to use it either. I doubt if many professionals would have such extreme 'over my dead body' views; nevertheless we will each have some degree of skew.

For me, denying that mental illness exists or that medicine has nothing to offer runs completely counter to my experience. Lunatic asylums may be dinosaurs, but to argue that residential treatment is inevitably bad is illogical. We will continue to need hospitals or something like them (though not necessarily adopting the traditional medical model: what about a health resort?) for three functions at least:

1. to deal with especially difficult instances of illness, whether acute or chronic, which demand intensive, multidisciplinary work from highly trained staff;
2. to add to the range of choice available for purposes of asylum or respite care;
3. to provide centres of excellence as the base for research, the development of practice, the advanced training of staff and to offer consultancy to other people and organisations.

In civil liberty terms, there has to be special provision for dealing with mental health emergencies, if nothing else, since the usual processes by which citizens are deprived of their liberty could not cope.

At the same time, these various movements have major achievements to their credit. We are beginning to listen to sufferers and to take their views seriously. We have begun to develop alternatives to hospital care and to get rid of the old psychiatric dustbins. We are thinking harder before we use the law to detain and treat ill people.

Disagreements within psychiatry about the origins of psychosis

For the dementias we have a clear organic cause for the condition even if we do not yet entirely understand the processes behind it. For schizophrenia we are still seeking an agreed physical basis and in the absence of definite evidence we are still arguing about it. For the affective psychoses we have some idea of the physical processes at work, even if we are still hazy about what causes them. The rapidly expanding field of genetics may help to throw light on some of these matters. Where we stand in the controversy is of real significance for our practice. Taking some of these divergent views and again reducing them to a simplistic absurdity in order to make my point, the logical outcomes lead in very different directions. (Siegler and Osmond, 1966.)

Views and outcomes

Szasz (1961) would deny that mental illness exists medically at all. We cannot establish a diagnosis by any clinical means; we have to rely on observed and reported behaviour. Behaviour is socially defined in that it is approved, tolerated or disapproved. This leaves psychiatry exposed to manipulation by social forces and becoming, in effect, part of the mechanism of social control. It was not that long ago in this country that we finally got rid of the 'moral defective' category in legislation which meant that 'promiscuity' or having an illegitimate child were grounds for detaining women in psychiatric hospitals for almost a lifetime. Szasz is absolutely right to warn us of the potential dangers to civil liberties. The ultimate logic of Szasz's argument would be the dismantling of all specifically psychiatric services and for all behaviour to be dealt with on its merits by other socially approved means.

Existentialists (such as Sartre, 1969) would appear to value human experience for its own sake. Arguably a psychosis is an extension of human experience and should therefore be valued. Using this rationale, a few, such as Huxley (1977) have gone as far as apparently to condone the use of drugs which produce quasi-psychotic symptoms. Without going this far, the valuing of experience would suggest that we should at least not step in to curtail it through, say, the use of medication. Intervention would only be justified where others' rights to live their own lives were seriously threatened.

Laing (1970) sees schizophrenia, at least, as the product of dysfunctional family interactions. The sufferer (the child) is caught in a double bind of conflicting overt and covert messages from parents. To obey one is to disobey the other, and the only way out of the dilemma is to retreat from an intolerable reality into 'illness'. Family group therapy therefore becomes the logical means of treatment.

Melanie Klein (Mitchell, 1986) sees mental illness as a regression. In the first few months of life a baby will move through a schizoid position (unable to distinguish between self and not-self), a paranoid position (distinguishing between self and not-self but seeing the latter as threatening and not yet personalised) and the depressive position. The infant is now aware of other people and begins to relate to them. This makes the infant vulnerable to others' approval. If they signal that they do not approve, the infant may introject this and feel worthless. Relations with the mother are especially crucial. Under pressure in later life, the sufferer may regress to that position which is supportable. As Donald Winnicott once remarked in lectures, you need to have had some mothering at least in order to be depressive. Klein's approach offers an interesting explanation of symptoms such as the loss of ego-boundaries in schizophrenia that some sufferers experience. The treatment logic of her ideas would be to accept the regression and, through another more positive experience of being parented, help sufferers pass through the succeeding positions successfully into a more resilient maturity. An account of this type of work is given in Barnes and Berke (1990).

Winnicott himself (1964), also from an analytic viewpoint, saw a value in depression which I have heard him liken to a fog descending on a battlefield. Activity is shut down to put energy into a conflict going on at the unconscious level. The conflict is about trying to achieve a new equilibrium in an old, ongoing war. Winnicott saw this process as typically healthy since the new accommodation would be more mature and constructive than the old. The intervention strategy then would not aim at stopping the fight (tantamount to an imposed armistice which would break down and lead to renewed hostilities), but would support the forces of maturation with psychotherapeutic help.

The organic school of psychiatry would see the psychoses as physical in origin. The process is not yet understood and could involve genetics, toxic conditions, biochemical malfunctioning or a disease process; but before long research will provide the knowledge we need to develop a cure. In the meantime we do have treatments such as drugs and ECT that are effective in controlling symptoms and help to restore social functioning, even if we do not always know quite how they work.

As the final example, there are the psychiatrists who acknowledge the probability of an organic basis to psychoses but consider the factors latent until triggered by stress. They would therefore see treatment as two-stranded: drugs and so on, coupled with other methods aimed at relieving the stress factors. This would require a multidisciplinary team approach. Unless both aspects were addressed, relapse would occur.

Choice of view

Which perceptions we use will profoundly affect the means we use and the ends we seek. My own base is the organic plus stress school, but with two qualifications. First, that other approaches have something to offer as a framework of understanding and a conceptual basis for our work. I have already mentioned Szasz and civil liberties; but from practice I can recall instances where I felt sure Laing was right, such were the family dynamics; and on other occasions I felt sure the organic school was right, since I could find no undue stress factor – the illness just happened. Second, whatever the precipitating stress, the illness itself creates stress for everyone concerned, not least the sufferer, which demands addressing in its own right. Arguably this area of stress has to be brought under control before any precipitating elements can be tackled.

In Figure 2.1 (p. 30) I endeavour to set out the structure of my approach utilising what has already been written and providing a framework for subsequent chapters. Diagrams have their limitations, however: critically in this one there is no mention of sufferers, families or carers and the centrality of their views and wishes in the process. I am also making the assumption that there is a sufficient coincidence of view in the multidisciplinary team for it to function adequately (elaborated in Chapter 5), while the structure is more particularly related to direct work with the sufferer. Aspects of practice considered in Chapters 6 and 7, for example, are only inferred here. I also need to explain my terms. By medicine I mean those physical treatments

Working with Mental Illness

Figure 2.1 *Structure of approach*

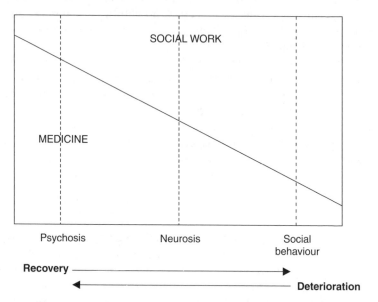

addressed to organic processes; by social work I mean the psycho-social means of addressing socio-emotional processes. I do not mean professions, staff, organisations or buildings, though I realise there will be general expectations about who does what, and where. Every-one involved needs to take both spheres into account anyway, and given the diversity of methods available within one profession or occupation and the blurring of practice distinctions it would be more helpful for the team to look at needs and the balance of inputs to meet them rather than to rigidly specify in advance who will do what. The two spheres are intimately interwoven in practice: if physical care is poor, the other therapeutic interventions are going to suffer; care, support and encouragement will need to accompany physical inputs if they are to be effective. In a residential setting, for example, whether the food is good or poor can have implications for the whole regime.

The arrows indicate the directional flows and the consequent changes in the balance of inputs. Examples might be the deteriora-tion in a progressive dementia – largely a matter of social behaviour in the early stages, but a matter of 24-hour predominantly physical care ultimately. Alternatively, with acute symptoms controlled or the psychosis in remission, the focus becomes the socio-emotional rehabilitation of the sufferer rather than intensive medical care. My position may or may not be acceptable to others, but we all need to identify 'where we are coming from' if we are to make any sense of what we are doing.

3

Practice Issues: Reflections from Experience

The genericism of mental health social work

Mental health social work is generic in that its basic aims are to reduce pain, relieve stress, offer practical services, bring in resources, restore social functioning, promote growth and development, speak up for the weak and powerless, protect the vulnerable and help people take control of their own lives. It has the same responsibilities to challenge social attitudes and the social policies and provisions which stem from them where these work to the detriment of clients.

Mental health work is also generic in the sense that any practitioner is likely to come across it, so it is important that teaching about mental illness should remain an integral part of the basic training of every social worker whether they become an Approved Social Worker or not (Crepaz-Keay, Binns and Wilson, 1997) A specialisation always runs the risk of becoming isolated and, since the client group we serve also suffers social isolation, mental health social work may need to be particularly on guard against separation from its professional roots.

Psychosis or not: the dynamics of deciding

Specialist or not, there are going to be times in every social worker's career when they have to ask themselves, 'Are there grounds here for thinking this is a mental illness, a psychosis?' and to act on the basis of the answer. The kind of scenarios I have in mind are where the social worker is called out to a previously unknown situation because someone – perhaps a relative or a GP – is saying there is or could be a mental illness involved. It might be an unknown situation referred for another reason, but when the social worker gets there s/he begins to suspect a mental illness element. It might be a known situation where there has been a development which now raises the issue in the minds of other people or the social worker. One way or another, the practitioner has to decide, 'Do I give credence to what other people are saying or not?', or 'Do I raise this issue myself?' The question may not be answered immediately, since getting the answer can take time; but ultimately a decision has to be made. The decision is crucial if there is any question of using statutory powers, but I would argue that the decision is vital anyway since how to help most effectively cannot be settled until it is made.

The social worker is not a diagnostician but s/he will need to satisfy themselves whether this is a mental illness or not. The evidence necessary for a decision may be readily available or it may have to be sought: it may come from inside or outside the immediate situation; it may or may not be reliable. Externally, a considered report from an experienced psychiatrist after a thorough examination would be virtually irrefutable; gossip from people down the road who have hardly ever met the family concerned would weigh very little.

The evidence from within the situation is likely to be complex, since it will be mixed in with the social and emotional dynamics of the family and other networks built up over possibly many years. Evaluation in the initial stages can be a difficult, delicate and time-consuming matter. The social worker is often called in at a crisis point and, even if this is not so, the advent of a social worker creates something of a crisis. In either circumstance, given the nature of crises, there can be heavy pressure on the worker for a fast decision which may have to be resisted. Individuals may be out to impress their views on this newcomer – especially if s/he is seen as a powerful person, important to get on your side if matters are to be resolved in the way you want. Attempts to manipulate the worker may be particularly strong where participants' views are divergent and feelings are running high. We may need to constantly remind ourselves that we are not seeing this family as they usually function, and we should not make assumptions on the basis of current performance: we need to find out what the pre-crisis patterns were.

In coming to an understanding of the dynamic factors which are pushing matters towards or away from a mental illness diagnosis, who raised the issue and why can be significant, especially where this was done precipitately and without a great deal of substance to warrant it. A member of the family might be frightened ('They are changing: illness is the only explanation; cure them so things can be as they were') or retaliating ('I'll get my own back for your behaviour towards me by calling it mad so you will be dealt with'); making a bid for power and control ('You are mad, cannot be taken seriously, so what I say goes now'); or defensively avoiding looking at themselves ('It's their problem, not mine'). Sufferers usually allow other people to refer them rather than refer themselves direct, but they can still be manipulative ('I am ill; now they will have to dance around me'); or be trying to escape responsibilities ('They can't expect this, that or the other of me: I am ill'); or indicating they have reached their limit ('I have had enough: someone else can take over now'). The great majority of families will refer from a genuine deep concern for the sufferer, and sufferers from a genuine fear of what is happening to themselves; but we need to be alert to other possibilities, even if they are far less common.

Conversely, we can examine why a referral was so delayed when someone had obviously been ill for some time:

> Mrs S. was admitted to hospital suffering from schizophrenia. From the social history it became clear she had been ill for some years but the family had protectively contained her. It was not until she had decided to leave home and live in an old chicken coop on the local allotments that the mental health services had been called in.

In many cases of dementia, it has been plain there had been increasing difficulties over months or years. Quite apart from a natural reluctance to 'see' mental illness in people we care for and an unwillingness to stigmatise them, I have often felt that people were reluctant to raise the issue for fear of starting a process over which they would lose control. While we may have a similar fear about physical illnesses, a mental illness is qualitively different in that something can be done about it by compulsion if necessary. This makes the professional strangers who come in to deal with it rather menacing: they have the power to tear away the person we care for, immure them in a remote, grim hospital and subject them to treatments we have heard awful things about. While for physical illness we may welcome the intervention that will restore our loved one to health, for mental illness we are much more ambivalent and some people will carry on coping until the situation becomes desperate (Howe, 1998).

I have long since been convinced that it is not the severity of the mental illness but the level of tolerance of the symptoms which is the crucial factor in referrals. We tolerate more from those we know, value and care for; much less from strangers and people we dislike. Mrs Jones can wander up the street where she lived for 30 years, chattering away to her voices and she will be greeted with sympathy. If a newcomer with the same symptoms were to move in, she would be ostracised and the pressure would rise to 'get something done' about her.

With sufferers, too, fears of unleashing uncontrollable processes and of stigma can hold them back from seeking help. Another possibility, however, given the nature of psychosis, is that the sufferer may have no insight into their condition, deny their illness or offer a variety of rationalisations for their behaviour, leaving the family (and the social worker) uncertain what to do. Even if they cannot accept the explanations, the family may recognise that to bring in the mental health services will be to create an enormous upheaval and they wonder whether this price would be worthwhile, especially if they are still clinging to the hope that everything may yet go away. Procrastination will account for the delay.

It may not always be the family or sufferer who precipitates or delays a referral. Professionals can care about clients, be reluctant to see psychosis, hesitant to set off a stigmatising process or create an upheaval that could have severe repercussions for their relationships. Conversely, suggesting a mental illness makes this a medical matter, offers symptomatic control to maintain a situation, and we have the defence of having 'done something'. At the same time we have avoided the demands that family therapy, behaviour modification or other methods would make of us. Under pressure, we might precipitate a referral as easier for us.

Perhaps our most agonising situation is where we know we ought to raise the issue but hesitate because we are aware of the poor quality of the services available. This is not to criticise the personnel of such services who may be only too well aware of the paucity of what they have to offer. There is still an overwhelming case for the reformist tradition in social work; and in conjunction with others to press for improvements in services to mentally ill people.

Crucially, for whatever reason or wherever it originates, raising the issue of a possible mental illness is the end of one process and the beginning of another. Understanding the lead-ups could be vital in shaping any subsequent patterns of intervention.

Psychosis or not: the outcomes of deciding

Having worked our way through the dynamic and diagnostic material we have gathered, we should be in a position to answer our question: is this a mental illness (psychosis) or not? How we answer is crucial in three respects: for the impact it will have on the current dynamics; its consequences for the handling of the situation and its outcome; and the implications for teamworking.

The impact on dynamics

We look here at some of the possible interactional consequences of raising the issue of mental illness. I am deliberately being gloomy to underscore my point about the significance of the decision.

To begin with, the mentally ill individual will have to be named and the named person may well reject the definition. Someone suffering from paranoid delusions will retain his/her conviction that their perceptions of reality are accurate and that people who suggest they are ill could be part of the plot against them. Someone accused of being forgetful may still argue they are not: other people are playing tricks on them or stealing from them. Even a sufferer with some degree of insight may resist the 'mad' label (as they see it) for reasons we have already mentioned and cling to other explanations for their feelings and behaviour. It is sometimes hard to convince someone suffering from an endogenous depression that they are ill. They take responsibility for the way they feel and think they should be able to deal with those feelings themselves. Whoever suggests to people they are mentally ill runs the risk that working with them subsequently could become very difficult. If the suggestion of illness originates outside the family and they all reject the definition and close ranks, the situation becomes virtually impossible to work with.

However, on the assumption that others are variously prepared to accept a mental illness definition, whether or not the named person does, there are a range of possible reactions to influence the interactional dynamics. I have in mind the myths, fears and fantasies associated with mental illness; there is enough of a grain of truth in some of them to mean they are matters which may well need to be dealt with (Heller *et al.*, 1996). They might have been around in the 'lead up' process, encouraging or discouraging a referral, say; or they might arise as the consequence of a mental illness possibility being raised. Either way, they are likely to be unhelpful and so become a professional concern:

1. *Insanity runs in families*. Depending on the generation involved, parents may be asking what might have been passed to their children and who passed it; or the children could be asking what they might have inherited from their parents and the consequences for them: their existing or anticipated marriages and children. Genetics are almost a popular science nowadays but with all the possibilities of a little learning being a dangerous thing. There are openings here for quite inappropriate guilt, blame and recrimination. If individuals or relationships are particularly vulnerable to these or they can be exploited in the context of already damaged/ damaging personal relationships, there may be some urgent social work to be done.

2. *Images of bizarre speech and behaviour*. Issues can arise, not only about actual behaviours, but about anticipated behaviours: the 'what if ...' syndrome. Reactions can vary: one possibility is withdrawal. In social interactions, if we do not get the response we expect, or if we are apprehensive about the response we might get, discomfort leads us to break off contacts. If this is not altogether possible then we reduce them and keep the person concerned at physical and emotional arm's length. Alternatively we can 'hover', keep the 'mad' person under surveillance and try to anticipate and control any potential eruptions of undesirable behaviour. Both reactions can represent a disturbing change in the existing pattern of relationships and interactions.

3. *Discounting*. A 'mad' person, being irrational, has no valid contribution to make. Any views they express can be ignored. Life is organised and decisions made without them: their place is to fit in. The preoccupation, solicitous indulgence and overprotection

which is sometimes the family reaction can also be a form of discounting, in the sense that normal expectations have been withdrawn and the sufferer is basically being treated as a small child: adult responsibilities are taken away. Institutionalisation is not confined to psychiatric hospitals. It can occur in people's own homes and for much the same reason – a way of managing the 'patient' that is comfortable for the 'staff'.

4. *The fear of violence.* This leads to humouring, placatory behaviour born of anxiety to keep things smooth, not to upset the ill person and so avoid explosions of temper.

5. *That mental illnesses are incurable* and that while there may be occasional partial remissions, the reality is that this is how things will always be. This perception, whether or not it is accurate in the circumstances, can colour people's approach and make them feel they are being pushed into a choice between shouldering the anticipated burden or putting their own interests first

The fears triggered by raising the issue of mental illness will be further complicated by the potential consequent social embarrassment (Sayce, 2000) The family reactions are likely to be replicated among kin, neighbours, friends, workmates and others, amplified by gossip and hearsay perhaps. The social costs of being mentally ill or having a mentally ill member of the family are high, and it is easy to understand why people devise more socially acceptable explanations and employ euphemisms such as 'nervous breakdown' in offering interpretations of what is happening to the outside world.

To try to protect their position, families will do their best to ensure that bizarre behaviour is not seen by others, even if this means restricting the sufferer's social contacts to those who are likely to be sympathetic and discreet. To do this will probably mean restricting their own, too. If people cannot be invited home, then invitations out cannot be expected or accepted. If people do not have a trusted 'sitter' they may not be able to get out at all, or only singly (Mace and Rabins, 1999). These social ramifications are bound to have their effects on the dynamics of the family and the dynamics surrounding the mentally ill individual. Frustration, isolation, resentment and the demands of care will take their toll, though the symptomatic expression of this will vary between individuals and in the same individual over time. People will grope for the most effective and comfortable way for them of handling matters.

Merely raising the mental illness issue will set people's thinking and imagination going. These anticipatory feelings, such as those outlined above, can be stirred into the current dynamics to compound matters. Besides these effects on relationships and interactions, raising the issue is likely to have further significant effects. Establishing the cause of the problem (mental illness) and locating it in a particular person also establishes that this is a medical problem beyond the competence of the sufferer or family to deal with. Treatment will be focused on the named individual, the responsibility for it vested in the medical team. The expected treatment will be by drugs but could include some time in hospital, then a rehabilitation programme. The patient will be expected to cooperate in the treatment prescribed by the professionals; the family will be expected to support the treatment programmes under the direction of the professionals. In effect we will have established a whole set of expectations, responsibilities, roles and relationships. Many sufferers and families may well welcome this framework; they will feel reassured that with the backing of modern medicine their situation will be restored to normal (or as near normal as possible). What may remain questionable is the appropriateness of this 'set' to the nature of the problems.

Oddly, this 'set' will make the psychiatric team vulnerable. If the treatment does not produce the expected outcomes, families and carers (as well as the sufferer) will have someone else to blame. At one extreme this may be a projection to mask their own reluctance to contribute what was needed from them; more possibly it is a reflection of a misjudgement somewhere of what they were able to contribute. More was asked of them than they could sustain. It could also be an accurate view of the failure of the psychiatric services. Too many families and sufferers have been forced into fighting for appropriate treatment, coerced almost into an antagonised rather than a cooperative stance (Rogers *et al.*, 1993; Neale, 1998). None of this is helpful.

It will be rare for the social worker to raise the question of mental illness: it is far more likely that someone else will have raised it and that some of these very powerful processes will have begun by the time s/he arrives. The issue then becomes one of endorsing the diagnosis or not, and of dealing with the processes in the light of that decision. Many of the processes can be damaging whatever the decision.

The consequences of the decision

When confronted with the question, 'Is this a psychosis or not?' it is crucial we get the answer right. To illustrate my point let us imagine the case of a woman referred for depression where we ultimately have to choose one of two working hypotheses: that she is suffering from an endogenous depression or that this is a matter of family dynamics and she is carrying the symptoms of a malfunctioning family system.

Calling the depression endogenous when it is a matter of dynamics will mean a symptomatic treatment of the woman, probably with anti-depressants. Additionally it could trigger some of the reactions mentioned above and provide an authenticated reason for the family members to say, 'This is her problem, not ours; it is for the doctors to cure, not us.' The real cause of her depression is untouched and her position as repository has been reinforced. To try to subsequently change tack and introduce, say, family therapy as the method of choice to tackle the real problem of dynamics will now have the additional hurdle of the triggered reactions and defensive let-outs to overcome, besides the resistance to be expected anyway. The chances of success are much more remote.

On the other hand, attributing the depression to dynamics when it is endogenous can be equally futile. The family could be in therapy for months with no substantive change. This lack of progress is likely to make everyone depressed, let alone the sufferer whose condition may be made worse by feelings of guilt about what is happening to the rest of the family. The suicide risk could be increased and possibly tip over into a bid, or worse. This would be a tragedy in any circumstances, but one heightened here because the appropriate treatment should have prevented it. Changing the treatment would probably be easier in this instance despite the resentment about what the family had been put through unnecessarily.

There are other situations where the decision, mental illness or not, would be equally crucial. Is this rather exaggerated adolescent behaviour or is it prodromal schizophrenia; are these eccentricities of age or are they symptoms of dementia? The decision is going to be a matter of deep significance, not to be arrived at lightly. We need to be as sure of our ground as we can given the outcome consequences for everyone concerned.

The implications for teamworking

Getting the decision right is essential if the subsequent treatment programme is to have the best chance of success; but almost equally important is getting the decision accepted. The ideal situation is where the three parties – the ill person, the other participants and the professionals – are agreed about what is 'wrong' and how they are to go about putting it 'right'. We have seen some of the difficulties there can be in establishing a concordance and the best we may achieve is an agreement to disagree, but with enough common ground to enable the next few steps to be taken before renegotiations begin. It has long been a function of social work to be particularly responsible for getting a sufficient degree of cooperation for work to get started and then maintained. If there has to be a starting-point for this, my choice would be to secure enough agreement among the professionals involved since it is difficult to see how meaningfully either the sufferer, family or anyone else can engage until this is established. Presenting them with a confusion of disagreements can only make their situation worse.

This process of securing agreement among the parties can smack of organising a conspiracy against the designated sufferer, and while it may not be possible, given the nature of psychosis, always to gain cooperation, much of the consumer antagonism must be due to poor practice. No-one, whichever party they belong to, is going to like being dragged along at the behest of others; least of all the sufferer, who has the most to lose, after all, from reputation to freedom. Even if we start with the professionals, we must recognise that the most important agreement to secure is that of the sufferer. We can best achieve this if we begin with their views and wishes and ask ourselves whether we can justify modifying them in any way.

4

Working with the Sufferer

In this chapter the face-to-face transactions between the person with the mental illness and the social worker are considered, and in the following two chapters transactions between the social worker and others will be addressed. Obviously the two situations are not distinct, but experience suggests that this is a reasonable basis for organising the material. This part of the book rests on the assumption that a diagnosis of psychosis has been made and accepted, at least as a working hypothesis by the people concerned. Comments are grouped around a series of working axioms considered to have a validity, whichever psychosis is involved. They are seen as a means of analysing what a social worker could or should be doing, and as a way of giving direction and purpose to intervention.

Axiom I: empathise with the sufferer's reality and the responses it generates

Exploring the sufferer's reality

Earlier, psychosis was characterised as involving some degree of loss of contact with outer reality and a response to an inner reality. Here I am thinking particularly of empathy with that inner reality which is obtruding – sometimes to the point of dominance. There are many accounts written retrospectively by sufferers themselves (Howard, 1988; Styron, 1991; Rowe, 1988, 1996; Watkins, 1996; Rogers *et al.*, 1989; Wing, 1983) which can help us to understand the experience of being mentally ill. Research into causation (Pritchard, 1995) and literature can also help: novels (Galloway, 1990; Bernlef, 1988) as well as the Bible and Shakespeare, poetry and music (Prins, 1986). It can be hard for us to imagine a world so terrifyingly dark, with a never-ending despair, that it becomes unendurable and the only relief is to escape through death. Even worse, if that is possible, is the depression accompanied by a sense of doom so horrible that it becomes an act of love to destroy one's children to spare them from what is coming before killing oneself.

People with paranoid delusions must feel perpetually hunted. They can never be sure of anyone: stranger or close friend may be part of the conspiracy to poison their food or gas them as they sleep. Auditory hallucinations in which the sufferer is the sole topic of a denegrating, sometimes obscene and always unstoppable conversation of disembodied people in his/her head would make most of us scream. How could we face anyone if we were convinced everyone around could hear what we are thinking? Visual hallucinations must be even more frightful to bear if they embody some of our most profound and secret horrors. The sheer chaos of an acute hebephrenic schizophrenic episode would understandably reduce us to frenetic random activity or cowering immobility.

There are some accounts of the experience of dementia (Leslie, 1991; Goldsmith, 1996) but there are also telling accounts of the process by caring family members (Grant, 1998). My own mental imagery is of being in a strange building where every door leads into a room, a corridor, perhaps a garden or a street which I have never seen before. The place is populated with strangers, though some of them pretend they know me and try to shepherd me to different places I do not recognise. No-one listens to me or understands me when I ask to be taken back to my own home. I worry increasingly that my family will be expecting me and that I shall be letting them down by not being there. The family and my friends seem to have abandoned me: they do not come to see me, but I comfort myself by saying that they will soon. As this process goes on, I swing between getting furiously angry and hitting out, searching for the familiar, or breaking down in tears of utter misery and despair. My last resort will be resignation and a descent into apathy where even the effort of trying to stay alive seems no longer worth it.

Perhaps the exception among the psychoses is mania, characterised by a feeling of supreme well-being. Everything I say is clever and witty, all my schemes are sure-fire winners, money is no problem whatsoever, so I can splash it around as I wish. Socially I am the most popular person about and a smash hit with members of the opposite sex. I get furious with people who try to thwart me, but my bad temper never lasts long and I can get on with the multitude of things there are to do. My head is bubbling with ideas and there is no time to waste – especially on yesterday's 'old-hat' notions. With thoughts of this kind, understandably sufferers cannot be convinced they are ill until they virtually collapse with exhaustion from increasingly frantic activity and lack of sleep.

The basis of empathy is listening and sending back the message that the communication has been received and understood. If we remain unsure we look for clarification and check we have got it right. Some sufferers, though, with their ability to send and receive messages disrupted, may not be able to assist clarification very much. We may have to use what information we have, together with our experience and imagination, to try to construe what people are trying to say. Meacher (1972) and Good (1989) demonstrate how these skills can be used to comprehend what confused elderly people might be struggling to convey.

The functions of empathy

Empathy has several important functions:

- First, *it helps to gauge where the boundaries of the illness lie.* Depression is pervasive and undermines our capacity to function over many areas of life, while suicide is always a risk to be taken into account. What the sufferer can reasonably sustain despite the illness and the degree of risk of suicide will be important factors in planning our work. Many people suffering from paranoid schizophrenia will have intact personalities, so the focus of our concern can be the delusions and/or hallucinations: their form, degree of intensity, extent and how the sufferer is managing them. If personality functioning has also been affected by the ill-ness then, clearly, more is going to come within the ambit of concern. With dementia we may have to make a similar kind of distinction: is this a matter of memory loss only, or is there some accompanying personality deterioration also? Even the communication difficulties will be telling us much that is relevant.

  Establishing where the illness boundaries are is important in helping us to avoid blanket assumptions (or accepting other people's) in terms of what sufferers can or cannot achieve. To take over more than is absolutely necessary from ill people is not only an uneconomic investment of time and effort, but risks generating dependency – or provoking resentment of an infantilising intrusion.

- Second, *empathy will add to our understanding* of what is going on inside this person, which can be important for several reasons:

1. There may be a logic to be found in apparently bizarre behaviour, provided we can appreciate to what it is a response. We are typically more tolerant of behaviour we can understand and not only can this help our own work but, through interpreting behaviour to others, we can add to their understanding and tolerance, contributing to a general easing of pressures and tensions.
2. Understanding will help us to identify what we need to address and give us ideas about priorities. If someone is on the verge of suicide this obviously becomes first priority. If someone is on the point of acting upon their delusions in a way which will inevitably bring trouble for them, something needs to be done urgently. A client was referred to us once because he had put a brick through the window of a butcher's shop, under the delusion that the proprietor was selling him poisoned meat. Although the police took no action, his illness was now in the public domain with all the social consequences.
3. Understanding should give us pointers to what the sufferer might find easier or more difficult to accomplish and so suggest a sequence. Success with the easier would be a boost to tackling the more difficult.

- Third, *empathy can be therapeutic in itself* in that it creates a climate in which the sufferer can feel safe to unburden what s/he is experiencing, bringing a sense of relief, helping to give shape and form to what is happening and beginning to bring matters under control. Coping capacity, hope, motivation and self-esteem are raised. Because we can be disturbed by the content of what the sufferer is revealing it is only too easy to shut people up in a variety of ways: by false reassurance ('I'm sure you will soon get over it'), by distraction ('By the way . . .'), by direction ('Don't think of these things'), by irritation ('Pull yourself together'), by disparagement ('Nonsense'), by switching off and not listening, and by finding excuses to leave. Ill people will have experienced most of these from others; that you respond differently could be of great significance for them. It will be especially important not to appear frightened of what they are telling; to do so will only confirm to them that their situation is out of anyone's control and even more desperate than they thought. Staying with them and not panicking will offer the hope that they too can achieve mastery over what they are experiencing.

- Fourth, *empathy will help to foster the relationship between sufferer and social worker*. Sharing the experience of the illness will help create a bond of importance to subsequent work together. Even in dementia the relationship is of real significance (Zgola, 1999).

Getting people to talk is not always straightforward. Some may not want to reveal the extent of their illness. A few people with depression will assure others that everything is fine since they are afraid that if they were to disclose how they really felt, they would be overwhelmed or they would land themselves in a psychiatric hospital, their 'madness' confirmed. Such sufferers will need support and reassurance before they are able to be open. Others may hide their symptoms to manipulate others. Some of my nursing colleagues would tell of patients with depressive or paranoid symptoms who became very adept at acting normally in order to get their discharge from hospital. Others will deny they have any symptoms whatsoever: they fear what an admission might bring. Some of the saddest instances of denial from my practice experience have involved husbands with delusions about their wives' infidelity. While the team had little doubt as to the real situation, often there was little we could do to change matters, voluntarily or compulsorily, since basically it would be a case of one person's word against another's. The wife leaving was not always the end of the matter if her husband continued to pursue her; while knowing her husband was ill sometimes made it more difficult for her to leave – it was not his fault and he needed her care.

Other people with a mental illness who would not find it easy to talk would be those with retardation as a feature of their depression and those experiencing loss of volition, poverty of thought and flatness of affect as symptoms of their schizophrenic illness. The 'glass wall' which seems to surround some schizophrenia and dementia sufferers is also very difficult to penetrate. On the other hand, there may be times when we risk over-empathising. It can be easy to be caught up in a manic or depressive mood and to lose our objectivity in the process. It may also be better sometimes not to let the sufferer talk at length if they are getting increasingly agitated in the telling or becoming increasingly preoccupied with their internal world.

Even if we do not always succeed in establishing empathetic communication with the mentally ill person, it is important to try, if only to demonstrate that we care about what s/he is experiencing. Moreover, a failure to indicate that they have received our communication does not necessarily mean they have *not* received it. My older nursing colleagues would recall examples of sufferers from (now rare) catatonic schizophrenia who, despite apparently being totally withdrawn and giving no sign of being aware of what was going on, would on recovery be able to describe in detail earlier events.

Axiom II: help the sufferer to keep in touch with reality

It is important to try to limit the deleterious effects of the psychosis on the individual and his/her social functioning. In doing so we shall also be securing the base for recovery work – extending the grip on reality and reinforcing control over symptomatology. As a process, medication should have helped to initiate this but the resources of the sufferer also need to be marshalled to secure progress to recovery.

Much of what I have written elsewhere could have been included here; sustaining a daily routine, for example (see Chapter 6), has much the same objective. Two practice points should be made at this juncture:

Avoiding further confusion

To go back to Axiom I, empathising with the sufferer's reality is to be distinguished from entering it – in effect creating a quasi *folie à deux* which strengthens the influence of the inner (un)reality. True folies are rare, but those who have tried to deal with them will know how powerful they are, as in the following box.

While professional staff would not get into a true folie, there are considerable temptations to collude at times. It will seem easier to concur with a sufferer's illness-rooted ideas than risk an upset by appearing to contradict them. Rather worse is the temptation to exploit those ideas in order to achieve one's own ends. I wonder how many elderly ladies have been taken into hospital thinking they were going

> Miss C. had given up college to return to live with her mother after her father had despaired and left. The couple lived in the basement of their large, dilapidated house among grubby furniture and heaps of old newspapers, the sink piled with dirty crockery. There was no electricity, only gas. The couple were totally socially isolated: mother never went out; the daughter only to shop. Mother had suffered from schizophrenia for many years but refused treatment. Miss C., too, refused any intervention that obtruded into the pattern of life they had established together.

on holiday or to see a relative. It is no surprise that they sometimes never trust anyone again, especially the person who misled them.

It is perfectly possible to respect another's (inner) reality but at the same time to gently maintain that it is not a reality you share: that you see things differently. Not only is it professionally honest and ultimately the soundest basis for a working relationship, it is also arguably the best way to help the sufferer. If we do not distinguish between realities, they are going to find it more difficult to establish a distinction from which to learn to manage their symptomatology more effectively. The alternative is that the symptoms dominate them. We are really talking about empowerment: trying to enable people, not illness, to take charge of their lives.

Developing strategies for controlling symptoms

Many sufferers will have developed strategies of their own and need little from us except supportive encouragement. How they manage can provide valuable suggestions for other people. Sufferers from recurrent depression or mania will frequently recognise when they are sliding into another episode and get themselves back onto medication. For others it will be a question of identifying which aspects of their illness are presenting the acutest difficulty, what they find the most trying situations or times of day; then experimenting with different strategies to see which is the most successful for them. It is here that complementary approaches may be of real value, and there would seem to be three main groups of these:

(1) Those that seek to promote well-being generally (MIND, 1995; Mental Health Foundation, 1998); including relaxation and meditation (Fontana, 1999), reflexology, massage, reiki, accupressure (Mitchell, 1999) and aromatherapy (Lawless, 1998).

(2) There are also a wide range of texts offering practical guides to assist the management of symptoms: manic depressive disorders (Varma, 1997), depression (Atkinson, 1993), auditory hallucinations (Romme and Escher, 1993), anxiety (Kennerly, 1997), panic (Silove and Manicavasagar, 1997), stress (Charleworth and Nathan, 1997), breakdown (McCormick, 1997), low self-esteem (Fennel, 1999) and anger (Lindenfeld, 1993) among them.

(3) Means of self-expression such as drawing, painting, drama, poetry, creative writing, sculpture, photography, music, and so forth. These creative activities have a general value in themselves as a source of a sense of achievement, as a boost to self-esteem and as a means of demonstrating to others that, despite illness, sufferers can make a worthwhile contribution to society, countering stigma and social exclusion. Expression may be of specific help when it provides the opportunity to illuminate the experience of mental illness itself, and in giving it form to assist the process of bringing it under control.

It was interesting to notice through a connection with the National Lottery MIND Millennium Awards scheme (MIND, 2000) how many of the applications related to provision in these expressive areas for people with problems of mental distress, indicating a real consumer demand for the benefits to be derived from them.

While a variety of means will play its part in enlarging symptom management, more will depend on the sufferer's persistence. Our support and encouragement will be important in this. Work will be difficult with people who have little insight or who are severely depressed, suffer poverty of thought or considerable confusion, but by no means impossible.

Sometimes it will not be the illness which is the block to progress, but the medication. It is sometimes difficult to balance the control of florid symptoms with the effects of heavy sedation, but either can be a hindrance to self-management and call for a review. From some users especially (though not exclusively), there has been severe criticism of the way drugs can at times be used in psychiatric practice (Rogers, Pilgrim and Lacey, 1993; Breggin, 1993); in manners which may be ill-informed, indiscriminate, addictive, administered in hazardous combinations, in doses which far exceed those recommended, or with distressing side-effects and disastrous long-term effects. As mentioned earlier, they can be given against a person's will in certain circumstances. Rarely are sufferers given the full picture, allegedly, to enable them to make an informed judgement about accepting or rejecting them. The difficulties of coming off medication (Tricket, 1998) indicates the care that is needed in putting people on it. The exercise of patient choice can be crucial to motivation, to cooperation generally and persistence in particular.

Clearly, such criticisms are not going to be true in every case, but the possibility of their relevance needs to be borne in mind and addressed as necessary like any other feature that may hinder rather than help. It is not easy, however, to appear to be challenging another professional in his/her sphere of responsibility. This matter will come up again in the next chapter.

Axiom III: relate to the person, not the symptoms

People who are mentally ill present a fractured, distorted picture of themselves compared with their pre-morbid personality. Whatever the commonality of the symptoms which enables a diagnosis to be made, they are always individually expressed, their form and content reflecting the unique personality, experience and circumstances of the ill person.

Acquaintances, people encountered in daily living in shops or bus queues, can be very disconcerted by aspects of the sufferer's presentation. If, as they walk along, they are having a vociferous argument with people who (to the observer) are not there, others are going to back away, politely or brusquely. Depressed people, those with odd thoughts or mannerisms, or those who fail to recognise old friends, are not likely to be popular even within their established social circle. Constantly to experience social rejection must be extremely distressing. It can also lead into the sort of vicious circle Josephine Klein (1960) has been heard to describe: inappropriate behaviour leading to social isolation which adds to social hunger and drives people into even more inappropriate behaviour as they attempt to satisfy that hunger. It is essential that no social worker repeats and reinforces this cycle, and does his/her utmost to reach behind the symptoms and make contact with the person. To do so will be therapeutic in itself and vital for empathy, understanding and establishing a working relationship.

Finding and relating to the sufferer can sometimes be hard in practice. Depressed people are inevitably self-preoccupied and even to relate to another person takes much effort which cannot always be sustained for long. A person suffering from mania may be full of bonhomie but is quickly distracted. With the 'glass wall' of some schizophrenia sufferers or the vacancy of some dementia sufferers you may not feel you are really in contact with them at all. It is essential to act as though you were. Also difficult is the dementia sufferer who does not remember you from one occasion to the next. A photograph for the mantelshelf might be more use than the traditional calling card. The relationship with the sufferer (which is essentially what we are trying to edstablish here) is as important in work with a mentally ill person as it is with any other client. We may not always be able to establish it; but without it we are handicapped and reduced to working through the sufferer's environment only, not directly.

Axiom IV: promote the sufferer's skills to manage themselves and their lives

In analytic terminology, we are promoting ego-functioning. This will be approached in two ways: in relation to the unconscious and to the conscious.

Handling unconscious material

First, it has been my experience that people suffering from psychosis have produced more than usual amounts of unconscious material. In schizophrenia, for example, the content of hallucinations could suggest repressed material:

> Mrs H. was a gentle lady in her mid-50s, who had been very strictly brought up – the only child of a rigidly Victorian couple. She had cared for them until they died, but had eventually married at the age of 48 on a companionate basis. Her auditory hallucinations were full of sexual matter, much to her distress; and her voices accused her of being a prostitute.

Depressed people in their search for causes for their feelings can sometimes bring out deep, long-standing but long-forgotten conflictual material:

Mrs D. suffered a depressive episode. In interview, when the depression was at its worst, she would scream, stamp her feet and bang her fists in anger about her mother's preference for her elder sisters and their exploitation of this during her infant years. Ordinarily her relationship with her mother and sisters was close and supportive.

With dementia also, as personality crumbles and social restraints erode, the libidinal drives can become more coarsely apparent.

There can be a number of ways of construing this phenomenon. For me, one of the functions of the ego would be to keep this unconscious material at bay. Under the additional pressure of illness, however, the ego is stretched and this material begins to seep into consciousness. 'Deep' casework was at one time seen as the most prestigious social work activity and to get unconscious material to work with was a sort of professional feather in one's cap. In my view, the temptation to explore such material in a psychotherapeutic fashion with people suffering from a mental illness should be resisted. In the earlier years of psychiatric social work some members of the profession felt it right to undergo an analysis in order to be more effective practitioners, more self-aware. I knew mature colleagues who found analysis profoundly disturbing. I found it bad enough, in training and after, to become unpleasantly aware of aspects of myself that obtruded detrimentally into my practice. To use my construct, if the ego is already stretched by illness and exploring the unconscious puts further pressure on it, there is a real risk the ego will disintegrate.

My own approach was to accept this material, not to be frightened by it (since this would only confirm the fears the sufferer already had about what s/he was experiencing) but not to go into it. It was also my experience that, as people recovered and ego strength was restored, this unconscious matter typically returned whence it came and again was 'forgotten'. There were just a very few people who, when well, could look back on their illness and learn from it as an analysand might, using it as a growth experience; but 'Don't dabble with the unconscious when people are ill' would be my general view.

Strengthening conscious processes

By conscious processes is meant broadly the social and practical skills which enable us to survive in modern society and to derive a sufficient degree of satisfaction from life. Where people have suffered a relatively short acute episode of illness from which they have made a good recovery, they will have largely retained their skills, if not their confidence. They may need help to restore their self-esteem and to resume their place in their social networks. One of the commonest feelings people have after a period of illness is that of being a failure: that they have let other people down and let themselves down.

One of the crucial factors may be getting the formerly ill person back into the roles and responsibilities s/he held prior to the episode, especially during that awkward convalescent phase where people hover between being really ill and really well and are unsure what to do for the best. Some nice judgments have to be made about the pacing of the resumption, not only by the sufferer but by family, carers and professionals too. However, there may be some other processes at work to disrupt the pacing.

Defensively, everyone may want to 'forget the whole thing'; rushing back to normality assists this process – whether or not it is a realistic course. This could be happening, I felt, when people made it immediately clear that any follow-up from a hospital admission would be unwelcome. Among other patterns could be a smouldering resentment ('I've had it all to do, while you've been ill; now it's your turn') which could push more onto a recovering person than s/he could reasonably carry at that point. Conversely, matters can be slowed down: a spouse could have enjoyed their new responsibilities and be reluctant to give them up; a parent may have enjoyed having a 'child' again and hang on; a sufferer may have enjoyed being dependent and is loth to resume responsibilities. There may be work to be done to restore a more healthy equilibrium. Professionals, too, may enjoy clients' dependency, their company, or keep in touch, thinking they are indispensable. They may also be glad to see the back of some people. None of this really helps.

Where the illness is lengthy, handicapping or leads to deterioration, the problems associated with practical and social skills may be different. There are perhaps four ways of looking at them:

1. *Preventing.* We will lose skills if we do not practise them. It is important to review the sufferer's daily living patterns with him/her to ensure that skill-practice opportunities exist. Social isolation and unnecessary dependency on others in practical matters would be worrying features needing to be addressed.
2. *Sustaining.* In some conditions, mainly the dementias, skills are likely to erode as part of the illness process. The task becomes to sustain them as long as possible and reinforce them as they begin to fail. Visual aids developed to maintain orientation to day, date and location and aids to ensure medication is properly taken would be examples of supplementing short-term memory loss, say.
3. *Compensating.* We might compensate the loss of some skills by reviving others that may have been dormant over many years but remain intact. A good social history or memories thrown up by reminiscence therapy could provide ideas for alternative ways of enhancing dignity, self-respect and independence.
4. *Renewing.* Renewal equips people with the social and practical skills they need for self-sufficiency but which they have lost or never possessed. I am primarily thinking of the rehabilitation and discharge of long-term hospital patients typically suffering the effects of a chronic schizophrenic illness and/or institutionalisation; but we need to keep in mind that hostel and even home life can be stultifying at times and create similar needs for the renewal of skills. This sort of rehabilitation is almost inevitably a long process and there may well be limits to what can be achieved. It is to be hoped that prolonged rehabilitation will become a less frequent task if we can prevent the chronicity associated with past years.

These four approaches are likely to be more successful from a community base, utilising normal social processes and facilities. They are much more difficult to achieve from an institutional base: an artificial construct materially, geographically and socially. The implications of this for the structure and content of services to mentally ill people are far-reaching.

No distinction has been made here between social and practical skills since they are fundamentally inseparable (Seed, 1988). While it is possible to think of some practical skills we can carry out in isolation (domestic tasks if we are living alone), there are few social situations which do not call for practical skills, if it is only in the way we present ourselves: clean, appropriately dressed and so on. In dealing with money, shopping, visiting the pub or using public transport, we need to know how the cash dispenser works, the what, where and budget implications of buying, the when and where of the bus service, in parallel with the ability to read social situations and respond appropriately in terms of speech, touch, eye contact and the many subtleties which mean social acceptability and the furtherance of even our practical aims.

Implementing skills programmes

Skill maintenance and/or renewal do not necessarily have to be undertaken by professionals. We pick up many daily skills informally as we go along, and there is no reason why people recovering from a mental illness cannot use the same means, provided they have the capacity and opportunity. Only when we are sure that they do not, do we think of setting up something special. Even then, if we can get ordinary people with the 'know-how' to provide the necessary 'teaching', so much the better: it is economic of professional time, but, more importantly, it is normalisation in action and probably for the sufferer a more acceptable form of help, since it is less stigmatising. Befriending schemes come to mind here (Parish, 1998) and, perhaps even better, self-help groups (Wilson and Myers, 1998).

A more consciously professional input is required when the work will be extensive, intensive and require specialised knowledge, methods and facilities and a range of skills beyond the usual (Bellack, 1997). The fieldwork function is to assess the skills which need to be practised, reinforced, compensated or acquired and then to see the sufferer gets the help s/he needs. Some of that help may come from the fieldworker but the likelihood is that the sources will be many and various: day centres, evening classes, industrial rehabilitation units and employment training among others. The social worker's knowledge of resources is essential here, together with an imaginative view of how they might be used. In this sphere our occupational therapy colleagues will have much to offer.

Work on social and practical skills may be no quick or easy matter. It may involve a life review, tackling situational dynamics to remove blocks, identifying and bringing resources into play, supporting their engagement and sustaining their use until ends are achieved; but these are not unusual social work tasks.

Expectation levels

Crucial to these activities is where we pitch the level of expectation: too little or too much can be equally damaging. One leaves potential unrealised, the other invites failure; both are demoralising. The pitch needs to maintain a balance between hope (buoyed by demonstrable achievements), and pressure to attain further targets until the maximum possible degree of self-management is reached.

What an individual can achieve is not always easy to gauge. Firstly, it can be blurred by the sufferer's motivation. If we think someone is underachieving, we ought to begin by looking at our expectation levels and the methods, attitudes and relationships we are offering to make sure we are not contributing to it. Only after that should we take matters up with the individual concerned to see how their endeavours might be refreshed or redirected. On the other hand, we sometimes have people so keen to try that we let them take on tasks they cannot really handle at that stage with the real risk of a damaging setback.

Secondly, while we all have our 'on' and 'off' days, there is a complicating difficulty where people have a mental illness of determining whether the improvement or deterioration in functioning is a reflection of remission or development of the illness or whether it is a personal change for the better or worse. We may have to make a judgment here. If it is 'on' behaviour, we may be on relatively safe ground welcoming and praising the movement and seeing it as a plus for capacity and the subsequent programme. If it is 'off' behaviour (and we are sufficiently sure it is not anything we have contributed) we are faced with a choice: do we let matters slide as illness (for which the sufferer cannot be held responsible) or challenge them (as responsible)? In effect do we accept, albeit temporarily, a limitation of capacity or do we treat the 'off-ness' as an underachievement to be directly worked with? If the target, say, is to improve table manners to help reduce the social isolation that bad manners are generating, do we ignore slovenliness or not? If it is illness and we pick it up, we could be involved in a pointless altercation. If it is not illness and we do not pick it up, we have missed a chance to move towards our aim, perhaps. These are daily dilemmas many families, especially, face.

This is an area of practice where nursing colleagues, who have much more experience of long-term working alongside mentally ill people than the average social worker, have much to offer. Years back, most local-authority mental welfare officers were ex-psychiatric nurses anyway. This direct connection has been largely eroded with the coming of Social Services/Social Work Departments and their employment of social workers and the development of community psychiatric nursing by health authorities. I feel we now have to accept that to combine nursing and social work in one person is going to be exceptional and each profession will need to recognise and draw upon the particular expertise of the other as members of a team.

Getting the expectations right is important if the sufferer is not to deteriorate as a result of benign understimulation, or break down under a pressure they cannot sustain. Like all other assessments, expectations will need to be kept under constant review.

The social work skills

To draw this chapter to its conclusion, face-to-face work with mentally ill people is going to call upon all the social work skills. Basically the social work is the same as work with any other client, but my experience suggests, using Hollis' (1972) categorisation, that two aspects will be particularly exercised: the sustaining process and direct influence.

Sustaining includes interest and concern, sympathetic listening, acceptance, realistic reassurance, encouragement and the introduction of practical services. In situations which involve ongoing hard work on the part of the sufferer, the need for sustaining is evident, though I acknowledge that maintaining it can be wearing for the social worker and the team and a possible reason for the unpopularity of long-term work among some practitioners, regretfully. For them, the effort does not seem to be commensurate with the return.

Direct influence starts with the law, which gives us a right to intervene (on the assumption that people with a mental illness are unable to make decisions in their own best interests) at the point where illness puts them or others at risk. This right brings particular responsibilities both practical and ethical. All social work practice involves values and ethics (British Association of Social Workers (BASW), 1996; Clark, 1999; Tielveit, 1999), but practice in the mental health sphere brings them into focus particularly sharply (Dunn, 1998; Barker and Baldwin, 1991; Barker and Davidson, 1998)) mainly because, as approved social workers (ASWs) at any rate, practitioners are crucially involved in a legal process which potentially can deprive people of their liberty (or seriously curtail their liberty should they become subject to the proposed community care and treatment orders) without the intervention of courts/judiciary. Appeal systems do not come into play until after the event. The ASW will have to strike a balance between the rights of the individual and the rights of others in terms of the harm that might be done by the sufferer to themselves or others, once a diagnosis of a mental illness has been established.

In this situation, the ASW will be faced with making a judgement of the relative risks involved (Langan, 1999) while s/he is under a variety of pressures from other powerful sources, be they families or doctors, with different interests. They will also be under pressure from within, in terms of their professional objectivity, to avoid such elements as racism and/or sexism in coming to their judgements. Even if the social worker is not an ASW, the fact that they could alert a colleague who is will make some of this a potential element in the dynamics of even a non-compulsory situation. Similar ethical issues arise where a sufferer's capacity to manage their affairs comes into question. Though the harm can be physical, such as self-neglect, it is likely to be material as well.

The increasing support for assertive outreach measures to prevent people from falling through the net of mental health services is a clear use of direct influence to a degree that is rare in other spheres (Stein and Santos, 1998).

As ego-reinforcers, social workers could employ more directiveness than would typically be used in other kinds of work (with the exception of child protection work, perhaps). People with a depression will sometimes need a bit of a push to keep going. People with mania will need some reining in at times. Where poverty of thought and loss of volition are features of a schizophrenic illness, a good deal more initiative will be needed on the part of others while sufferers from dementia may need a practical framework of 'do's and don'ts' to survive socially and physically. These steps will call upon the social worker to

develop proposals and initiate actions within a purposive design even
if the means used are basically encouragment rather than instruction.

While some of our direct influence will derive from the law and
the position we hold in an organisation, more will depend on our
practice skills and the relationships we have formed. Lamb (1976)
identifies a series of principles on which long-term work with sufferers
from mental disorder should be based. Among them are a non-
institutional community base, using normalisation means in what
should be high-priority work; that high but realistic expectations should
be maintained; that the work should be with the well part of the self
and directed to clear goals, the most important of which is to give
sufferers a sense of mastery over themselves and their environment.
This succinctly summarises views that I share.

5

Working for the Sufferer: The Team

In this chapter and the next, we examine the social worker's activities on behalf of the sufferer. Again there are overlaps with what has already been written and what is to come in Chapter 7. The distinction I have tried to draw is between work for the sufferer which involves others, and work which stems from the needs of others, especially families, in their own right, leaving the latter till later. Indirect work for the sufferer I have divided into two: the responsibilities, functions and activities of the social worker *first* as a member of the clinical team, and *second* as having a particular responsibility for the interface between the person who is mentally ill and his/her environment; in other words, their social functioning – which is the focus of social work practice in any event.

The significance of teamwork

Teamwork has always been an essential element of good practice – that is, that which meets the needs of the ill person and their situation. As stated earlier, no one profession has the expertise or the authority to undertake everything. Teamwork has not always been easy: different organisational structures and finance, varying degrees of operational autonomy, different approaches and priorities have too often led to operational isolationism, professional rivalries, disagreements over issues such as confidentiality and complaints about practical issues – such as grumbles about what 'they' are not doing to the detriment of what 'I' am trying to do. A run of unsynchronised organisational changes have not helped. Local government boundaries and functions, care management, internal markets, the variety of National Health Trusts, Best-Value requirements, targets of many kinds, the emergence of primary care groups, contracting out and the developments in the private sector, among others, have been a destabilising backdrop whatever the good intentions were. The tragic consequences of the lack of cohesion have been spelled out time and again by enquiries into homicides involving mental illness issues (Parker and McCulloch, 1999; Ritchie, Dick and Graham, 1994) quite apart from users' experience. Bringing cohesion into the so closely interrelated health and social care services for people – not least, mentally ill people – has been a persistent theme of central government endeavours for many years (Dept of Health, 1993, 1995, 1997, 1998, 1999) culminating in the requirements of the National Service Framework (Dept of Health, 1999). These not only set out what should be available in the way of mental health services, but also how these should be planned, managed and reviewed – not just by public services but with representatives of voluntary organisations, users and carers. The development of partnership is now virtually compulsory: local plans that do not meet requirements will not be approved centrally. Financial inducements to support good practice, pressure to develop Social Care Trusts where services are not meeting targets, and the ultimate sanction of a ministerial 'takeover' of 'failed' authorities are now a real stimulus to local action. However, managerial plans are one thing and there may still be a need for work at the face-to-face level for aspirations to become a reality (Payne, 2000), but the prospects for multidisciplinary teamwork are probably better now than they have been for decades.

This chapter, oriented to teamworking, is built around two axioms: keeping the sufferer alive and contributing to diagnosis and treatment. Both have wide ramifications.

Axiom I: see the sufferer stays alive

By alive I do not mean just their physical survival, but their social survival also. I see this axiom as a primary responsibility that the whole team shares and one which profoundly colours their work. This immediately raises ethical issues connected to self-determination and the quality of life.

Self-determination: issues of ethics

For centuries the self-determination of people with a mental illness has been limited in the sense that procedures have existed to take decision-making out of their hands and give it to others – typically, as mentioned earlier, where ill people were deemed to be a danger to themselves or others, or incompetent to manage their affairs. The arguments have been about what constituted mental illness, where the behavioural limits lay and the procedures to be used with what safeguards to prevent abuse. Mental health policy and practice has always had to tread a fine line between mental health professionals (the 'treatment' lobby) and the human rights movement (the 'civil liberties' lobby) over the issue of protecting the vulnerable against the use of arbitrary power. The safeguards offered by the former are professional ethics; the safeguards sought by the latter are legal processes. The approved social worker is in a unique position: a member of one of the professions with power but charged with the responsibility to protect the liberty of the sufferer (Sheppard, 1991). His/her concerns are both ethical and practical.

I feel sure that if others were in real danger from someone with a mental illness any social worker would be ethically prepared to step in, compulsorily if necessary, to protect, say, the children of a depressed parent threatening to destroy them; or to safeguard someone who was the focus of paranoid delusional threats to life. The practical judgement involved would be gauging how real the danger was (Crichton, 1995; Kemshall and Pritchard, 1997; Prins, 1999; NACRO, 1998; Open Mind, 2000). Risk assessment and management is not an exact science, however. It is where we have failed to protect from violence, whether through a systems failure or a failure of judgement, that services have been publicly criticised (Zito Trust, 1993) and demands made for tighter controls over those deemed dangerous. Critics argue that much greater priority should be given by policy-makers and professionals to the rights of victims and potential victims of mentally disturbed people rather than those of the dangerously mentally ill. Conscious of this public pressure, the temptation to resort to defensive practice and err on the side of caution must be considerable. The potential for injustice, given this skew, is also considerable.

The issues are not quite so clear cut where the sufferer is jeopardising only themselves. The risks of self-harm in each of the psychoses are evident. With depression suicide is always a possibility, but not every sufferer will volunteer that they have suicidal thoughts, perhaps because they feel ashamed of them. I used to ask specifically about them, partly to clarify the degree of risk but also to signal that it was all right to talk about such thoughts; offering the opportunity for ventilation and considering how these thoughts might be managed. Even then, not all sufferers will acknowledge they have such thoughts. The old wisdom was that these were the patients determined to do away with themselves, keeping quiet so as not to alert others.

There is the view that people have the right to end their lives if they choose, and with depression they can appear to be more apparently rational in taking that decision compared with the other psychoses, given the despair that is such a feature of the condition. In my view it is still the illness which is selectively determining the decision, despite the presentation. Sufferers from schizophrenia can put themselves at risk responding to hallucinations and delusions, particularly in acute episodes. In torpor, self-neglect can also become a threat to survival, as can hazardous lifestyles (extreme reclusiveness, for example). Dementia sufferers can be at high risk from an unlit gas, an igniting chip pan, clothes drying over an electric fire, an unwitting overdose of medicine, wandering out onto a busy road and so on.

The protection of the life of the ill person is a clear justification for intervention and taking immediate safeguarding action including, as a last resort, the use of compulsory powers if necessary. The argument for this position is ultimately a moral one: the intrinsic value of human life. Rather more practical is the preservation of the opportunity for the sufferer to live a more satisfying life in the future: self-determined rather than illness-determined, with real choices, not illness-imposed ones; preserving their self-determination by intervention rather than robbing them of it. Substantiating my justification would be the people (and their families) who subsequently express their thanks to those who stepped in to give them the chance to resume their lives.

It is accepted that not all social workers will share my ethical perspective. The morality of social work has been widely discussed, but with only a limited consensus (Plant, 1970; Rhodes, 1986; CCETSW, 1976; Clark and Asquith, 1985, Tielvet, 1999). Nevertheless, the axiom has some further justification in that the public agencies which employ 90 per cent of social workers would expect us to work to preserve life, reflecting the public expectation that this is what social workers and others should do. This is at its most obvious in child care, though other vulnerable groups such as elderly, physically or mentally handicapped people also (rightly) excite public sympathy when social workers fail them. Sadly, in instances of mental illness, the illness *per se* seems to be a sufficiently satisfactory explanation for suicide. No-one else seems to be blamed by coroner, media or public enquiries to anything like the same degree. (The private self-blame of those who feel they should have been able to stop that suicide is another matter.) The fact is that a life has been lost, and some better practice might have saved it. That much suicide is preventable, given greater priority and improved practice, is now recognised and incorporated into NHS targets (Dept of Health, 1998).

Protecting life: the practicalities

From ethics, the preservation of life becomes a practical matter: ascertaining the risk and taking steps to minimise it.

- *Risk.* Risk in social work is a significant facet of the day-to-day experience of practitioners and managers. Where someone's life is in jeopardy we need to ask what is the nature of the threats to survival, where and when they are most likely to be at their strongest and what can be done to safeguard against them without offending the sufferer's dignity or robbing them of more self-determination than is absolutely necessary. A good many risks are practical, more especially for people suffering from dementia. Can we get power restored to get rid of the candles and paraffin stove? Is storage heating a possibility rather than an open fire; a kettle that switches itself off rather than one that goes on boiling? Would a pill-dispenser reduce the risk of an accidental overdose? Can sedation be justified to negate dangerous wandering at night? Occupational therapy has a great deal to offer in this sphere of practical environmental management. With depression and the risk of suicide, is it practical to limit a sufferer's access to medication to one day's 'ration'? A diurnal mood swing would suggest greater risks during the morning, while an anniversary with unhappy connotations might need two or three days of special vigilance. With schizophrenia it is perhaps more of a case of being aware when the sufferer is becoming more excitable or more lethargic, and being particularly alert.

Experience with the sufferer could suggest where more particular risks might lie.

- *Supervision.* At the heart of minimising risk is supervision, a term with rather unfortunate overtones, but I cannot think of a substitute. As an element of practice, supervision will become of greater significance with the introduction of any form of Community Treatment orders. While the risks (and the sanctions) will be greater, presumably, where an element of compulsion is involved, nevertheless the principles and practice will be basically the same whether compulsion comes into it or not. Clearly supervision in practice needs to be discreet and handled in a way which is, at the very least, tolerable for the sufferer. If it is pushed on people they are likely to resent it, reject it and vitiate its purpose. Ideally it should emerge as a byproduct of, say, family life, companionship, the delivery of a service, or the meeting of other forms of need. This may sound clandestine, but there is justifiable reason why when the more coercive alternatives in the absence of such opportunities are considered.

Little supervision will be necessary if the sufferer has some insight, knows when they are at risk and will get in touch with someone who can respond reliably and appropriately. One of the salient social work tasks is likely to be a review of the existing 'keeping an eye on' systems in the light of the identified risks, strengthening those systems where necessary. This may involve the introduction of new elements, but support and some relief for already functioning systems, coupled perhaps with some reorganisation and/or activating of existing potential, may be all that is required. For people in their own homes a combination from, say, family, friends, neighbours, volunteers, family aide, district nurse, community psychiatric nurse, GP and social worker could provide a system of cover as well as meeting the physical, social, emotional and practical needs of the mentally ill person. Bringing people into the home is not the only possibility: getting sufferers out to clubs, centres, shops and entertainments could serve a similar purpose. More extremely, day or night care might have to be used; as a last resort it might have to be residential care – a home, hostel or hospital – if this is the only way to get the cover the degree of risk calls for. In many cases this should only be necessary for short periods until the acute risk passes, or while the family caring for the sufferer has a break to enable them to subsequently continue to care.

Seeing that people stay alive is no justification for claustrophobic overprotection, which is both ethically and practically inexcusable. The only basis for taking control is that a person has demonstrably shown an insufficient capacity in that specific regard, and that the element is essential for their survival. The aim would always be to return control to the sufferer as soon as is reasonably possible. At its best, supervision is liberating, allowing people to remain in the freest circumstances with the most scope for making their own choices. If the resources can be mobilised, people can stay in their own homes: if they cannot, the social worker is faced with the stark choice of allowing risks that are not really manageable or organising residential care unnecessarily. Either way, the social worker will have failed to secure the legislative objective of providing care and treatment in the least restrictive way. The links between legal requirements, available resources and the ethics of practice are at their most demonstrable here. Sadly, while society may determine the ends, it does not always will the means: lack of resources may vitiate the legislation and good practice. When thought through, supervision can be one of the best defences against defensive practice, where social workers put their own needs for safety from possible criticism above the client's realistic needs for safety.

- *Networking.* Supervision is an aspect of networking (Seed, 1989), and three points should be made about this:

1. Networking takes time and resources – and not just those of the social worker: family, friends, neighbours, volunteers, voluntary and statutory agencies are all potentially involved. The necessary resources may or may not exist; they may or may not be creatable, especially in the short term. Even where they exist, negotiating and setting up communication systems may be difficult and protracted. Despite the original impression given, care in the community was never going to be a cheap and easy option. It will not properly exist as long as the principal facilities are based in hospitals and remain hospital-oriented, with services in the community primarily geared to emergency work. This will leave sufferers with what amounts to a shuttle service, in and out of hospital – neither ethical in terms of self-determination nor practical in terms of meeting needs.

2. It is crucial that we think in networking terms. It is only too easy to slip into the habit of seeing solutions in terms of the

services we have available: the problems are at night but we offer some home help time during the day because it is all we have. Until we start thinking more widely and more imaginatively, care in the community will remain stunted.

3. Networking has considerable implications for the way services are organised. If coordinating services (the formal and the informal) is a particular social work responsibility, then 'knowing your patch' is an essential, together with a sufficient autonomy of action and an adequate degree of authority over resource allocation. Some services have a tradition of professional autonomy and discretion and their patterns of organisation may be more suitable than, say, a local-authority Social Services department tending to bureaucracy. Community care can be under threat from more than a shortage of resources: the means of delivery can be crucial to producing the 'seamless robe' of the ideal service.

The quality of life

The preservation of life shades into the second area: that of the quality of life. Here there are perhaps two issues – are we preserving a life of such poor quality we could be said to be officiously keeping people alive; or are we so concerned for the quality of life (on which the bulk of social work is focused) that we are prepared to step in to maintain it even if this means using compulsory powers where we might?

Issues in preserving poor quality of life

These issues are more usually faced by the medical profession. Multiply-handicapped babies, accident victims on life-support machines, patients with terminal cancer, advanced motor neurone disease or multiple sclerosis must present doctors with acute problems at times, of whether to fight on with treatment or to let nature take its course, eased by 'tender nursing care'. There will be the rare occasion, though, where the principal professional responsibility will rest with the social worker. Do we leave this elderly lady suffering from severe dementia at home, despite the acute risks involved, when she is refusing to move? There may be little quality of life left, but would that to be found on a psychogeriatric ward be much better (Pink, 1990)?

Her life might be prolonged for a few weeks, but would this be to her or anyone else's benefit?

There are no easy answers: situations have to be individually assessed. If we reckon to be a profession then we must expect to have the responsibility of making judgments; otherwise we are only technicians going by the instruction manual. I can only suggest you gather your arguments after consulting all the people involved, talk it out with colleagues and seniors and come to a conclusion that would be defensible if you had to answer for it at an enquiry.

Issues in maintaining quality of life
There are obviously all sorts of ways in which people with a mental illness can damage their own interests and other people's even if these are not immediately life-threatening. People suffering from mania can destitute themselves and their families through wild spending, or strain to breaking point important relationships through their unreliability and/or heightened sexual behaviour. Depressed people in their search for reasons for the way they feel can blame job, spouse or neighbourhood; resign, divorce or move. None is a cure for the depression and they are now, additionally, unemployed, isolated or in debt, perhaps. People with dementia can, through their loss of capacity to make new memories, accuse others of neglecting them or stealing from them. As their personality deteriorates they can become quite vicious. One way or another they can drive away those they depend upon to continue to survive in the community. People suffering from schizophrenia, whether in an excited or lethargic phase, can end up getting sacked, put out of their lodgings or may get into a financial mess as a consequence of their behaviour. And some people with a mental illness are vulnerable to exploitation: protecting them can become another aspect of preserving their quality of life.

There is an endemic tension between the social work ethical principle that the client has a right to self-determination and our obligations to promote the client's best interests and see that others' interests are not infringed (Day, 1981). We know that, quite apart from ethics, self-determination is good practice. Decisions the client takes are much more likely to be implemented; imposed decisions are likely to be resented and subverted. To impose decisions, infantalises clients and reduces their capacity for self-direction; for them to decide for themselves promotes maturity. At the same time it would be most uncaring if we let a client go ahead when we knew that the decision or action would be highly damaging. We would use our best efforts to dissuade, and do so more strongly if we felt that other people's interests would be very detrimentally affected too. We care about them as well, since our caring cannot be selectively 'client only'. It is probable in such circumstances that the social worker will also be getting copious advice, if not downright pressure, from a range of people – kin, neighbours, other professionals, his/her own managers even – about what s/he should be doing. It is likely most of this would not be supporting self-determination for the client, but be of the 'do something' kind. In such situations it is difficult to be objective. It would help if we could sort out a basis for our own decision-making which would enable us to explain to others the rationale for our approach. Here there are a number of potential bases:

1. *To make a distinction between behaviour prompted by illness and that attributable to the person* (a point made earlier). In effect we would be saying that we would intervene where the sufferer was not culpable, but leave her/him to the normal social processes where s/he is culpable. While there might be occasions where this distinction could be clearly drawn, there would be many more which would be very cloudy. In any event, with 'sane' clients we do not leave volitional behaviour outside the scope of possible intervention and it hardly seems logical to do so in respect of people with a mental illness.

2. *To try to assess objectively whether the behaviour, and/or whatever lay behind it, came within the (wide) bounds of normality.* We would address the 'abnormal' and (apart from encouraging) leave the 'normal'. This would be akin to usual social work practice, but we know that to get a consensus on what is 'normal' in the circumstances is sometimes difficult, given the various subjective elements. Subjective expectations of mentally ill people could add an additional twist to the complexities. We may also sometimes confuse 'normal' behaviour with understandable behaviour. The understandable may still need to be tackled if it is damaging.

3. *To examine the range of means of intervention we possess,* from statutory powers (compulsory care and treatment, application to the Court of Protection, injunctions and so on) to the exercise of influence (whether by the negatives of threat or the positives of encouragement). We would ask ourselves whether they were available to us in the circumstances and then whether they could

justifiably be used (in the sense of avoiding sledgehammers to crack nuts, for example). We could finally ask whether they were likely to be effective. As previously mentioned, in the majority of situations only influence will be available to us. Its effectiveness will depend on the way people view the authority of the position we hold and the powers associated with it; the authority of our expertise and the respect our opinions command; and the kind of relationships we have and how valued we are – in other words how good our practice has been. Another approach might be to see if another figure in the situation has more influence than we have and get them to exercise it to the benefit of the aims of intervention. This could be asking much of them, though, if they take it on, and the support of the social worker in this task could well be crucial to its success.

Our reflections are likely to be influenced by the three 'golden rules': if you have a choice, use the positive rather than the negative means of influence; use the least coercive means available that will achieve the ends sought; and there is no point in making threats unless you have both the means and the intention of carrying them out if necessary. Behind our thinking will be some sort of hierarchy of means related to our perception of the seriousness of the situation. The complication here is that not everyone's view of the degree of seriousness is likely to be the same, nor their choice of how to deal with matters. Getting a sufficient consistency among those involved has to be a priority.

4. *To try to balance the advantages and disadvantages of intervention or non-intervention* in relation to the goals we are trying to achieve. Again this is no easy matter, since one person's advantage tends to be another person's disadvantage. We have already acknowledged some of the external pressures to which the social worker may be subject. There can be internal ones, too, skewing the perception of advantage/disadvantage: we may feel punitive or indulgent; we may be angry and disappointed when the sufferer apparently lets us down and a great deal of effort goes to waste; or there may be something about this person and/or their situation which stirs our need to protect and nurture them.

It is our responsibility to make decisions as objectively as we can: to be clear about the ethics involved, conscious of the extent and reliability of the information base we are using, alert to the interpretations we are making and sensitive to the feelings and reactions operating in the situation, not least our own. Our judgements about intervening need a base of substantiated plans geared to what we would like to see achieved by consciously considered means. We will need the skill to communicate our conclusions acceptably to others in order to work in cooperation with them if this is at all possible.

This chapter is concerned with teamwork, but in examining what may be involved in preserving life and its quality the potential range of contributors (the team, that is) can be extremely wide. The next axiom is more concerned with the clinical team and the social work contribution to it, but both teams are essential to the outcome and their collaboration crucial.

Axiom II: contribute to the diagnosis and treatment plan

These are medical terms and some colleagues will bridle at them, smacking as they do of professional domination of the pliant patient. However, in the Western world, doctors in general and psychiatrists in particular are seen as carrying the primary responsibility for dealing with sufferers from psychosis. As social workers in this sphere we cannot avoid becoming involved with medical practitioners and we need to be familiar with the way medicine thinks and works, and the language it uses, if teamwork is to be effective. We do not always have to agree: at times it may well be our responsibility to challenge medical practices from our own professional perspective. In the last resort, teamwork is essential if the range of needs in any one situation is to be fully met. Psychologists, nurses, occupational therapists, social care staff and others will be needed, in addition to medical and social work staff. Medicine would still be perceived as the leading, ultimately responsible profession – a sort of *primus inter pares*, to use a political analogy. To push the analogy further, in practice it is to be hoped that collective 'cabinet' decisions would be reached after full discussion with all those concerned and that these would recognise that, at a particular stage, the salient needs were within the competence of (a) particular professional(s) who would become the lead worker(s) for that period, with other professions working in support. As the needs changed so would the lead and support working. It is also to be hoped that the 'cabinet' operates democratically in terms of its 'electorate' – the sufferer and his/her carers – working to the mandate given to them, listening to and respecting this 'public opinion', and adopting their view unless there are powerful reasons against. The 'cabinet' should not need to be reminded that their electorate have other sources of appeal (MPs, councillors, Ombudsmen, Mental Health Tribunals, Mental Health Act Commissioners, the press and so on), quite apart from the 'ballot box' of voting with their feet, breaking off, and turning to other parties.

In exploring this axiom, what the social worker might contribute to the team process is examined under three heads: contributing to the diagnosis, knowing what the treatment programme is, and assisting its implementation.

Contributing to the diagnosis

There are two elements to this: contributing to the clinical diagnosis and to the social assessment:

- *Contributing to the clinical diagnosis.* The clinical diagnosis is important to us. We need to know and understand the features of the condition if we are to work effectively ourselves and collaborate realistically with everyone else involved. The clinical diagnosis is a medical matter but, in the course of our work when we come across information of significance for that diagnosis, it is crucial we feed this information into the team. A number of people first come the way of the psychiatric service in a crisis. By definition, a crisis is an exceptional state, but the professionals involved have to handle matters in terms of what presents and sometimes are obliged to act without the opportunity to get a clear idea of the background to the crisis. Other people caught up in it are not always in an ideal frame of mind for providing a clear, calm, accurate, reflective picture of the precipitating events either. In such circumstances it is possible to be misled. As a psychiatric social worker it was often my job to get this background and lead-up information by way of a social history, ordinarily from a close relative a day or two after the crisis, when the acute pressures were off. Even then information could be some time coming, especially if it was emotionally charged and the matter was difficult for anyone to talk about.

Social history taking has had its fashions, from never ('It is the patient's perceptions we are dealing with and any others are irrelevant') to always ('If we are to help this patient we need all the information we can get'). It also has many functions: it can be cathartic for the teller and of therapeutic value to him/her; it can help them put matters in a new, more constructive perspective; and it can help establish a positive working relationship not just with the social worker but the whole team. All help towards a better prognosis for the sufferer as well as a more accurate diagnosis.

Getting a history from a source other than the sufferer raises ethical issues of confidentiality (which apply to the getting of information, not just its passing on) but, given the nature of psychosis, the ill person may not be able to give a reliable account for some time, whereas something needs to be done quickly in terms of deciding on treatment. The history should help to ensure the treatment is appropriate. We should always ask the sufferer for permission to get a history. Where they can decide, I have rarely met with a refusal once the reasons have been explained: to enable the team to help the sufferer more effectively. Refusals we have respected, unless there was a medical imperative. Getting the history also shows relatives that the team consider they have an important part to play and so helps to establish a partnership based on mutual respect.

At times the history may be crucial to the clinical diagnosis. A confusional state which suddenly started three days before is not going to be attributable to a dementia: a steadily deteriorating condition over several months raises dementia as one of the possibilities. I recall getting the history of a lady admitted to hospital with a tentative diagnosis of hysteria, which clearly indicated a schizophrenic illness of some duration.

- *Contributing to the social assessment.* Understanding the personal, social and material context in which the sufferer's illness arose is almost as crucial as the medical diagnosis, since it will profoundly shape the processes by which this person is assisted to the best possible recovery. This is also information the team members will need to share on a 'need to know' basis, to recognise where their input relates to an overall strategy which takes the non-medical into account. In this area the social work contribution to the team is particularly significant, not just for the history but for the ongoing contact with home. The dynamics of the home situation are likely to be a matter of continuing change and the various team inputs will need to adapt if they are to be consistent with each other and the current position.

The aim of this axiom as a whole is to help establish an accurate, directed, coordinated effort. Too many sufferers and their families complain that they get utterly confused because the people they are involved with seem to have different notions of what they are doing and why. As a consequence they feel as though no-one cares or listens. We enter a deteriorating circle of interaction which will do nothing to assist anyone, least of all the sufferer. Establishing the clinical and social diagnoses should get the coordinated efforts away to a good start.

Knowing what the treatment programme is

The importance of knowing what the treatment is derives from three particular social work functions:

1. *The coordination of the teamwork*: seeing that the communication and decision-making systems are established and working, that information flows, that people know what they are doing within an overall scheme. A kind of secretarial function, as it were.
2. *Acting as the link person between the team, the sufferer and carers.* This will often involve the social worker as interpreter, explaining to others what the individual members of the team are trying to achieve from their different contributory positions.
3. *The link between clients and resource systems*, to use Pincus and Minahan terminology (1973). To fulfil this function we will need to know what systems exist, what they can contribute, their appropriateness and how to establish effective links with them.

Coordinating teamwork. Function (1) will demand a general understanding of the professional groups involved: their knowledge and skill base, their methods of working, the processes of the organisations in which they operate and so on. Too often professionals work in ignorance and isolation from each other, to the detriment of their clients. This is more true of community settings where people operate from different geographical locations and organisational settings, with different catchment areas and client orientations. We have had to invent systems to overcome this fragmentation, most noticeably in connection with child abuse. Joint Consultative Committees, jointly financed projects and joint planning for care in the community have helped to bring services together at one level; but they do not always seem to have made much impact at grassroots level. There we need complementary structures – and their antecedents, predisposing attitudes. My own feeling is that joint training represents one of the best ways for improving matters. For example, I would like to see all social work students undertake a placement in a clinical setting such as a hospital or multidisciplinary health centre. There is nothing quite like working in ongoing relationships, with clients/patients in common, from under one roof, to foster awareness of colleagues' disciplines. If the chance does not occur in basic training, then post-qualifying secondments and exchanges would be an alternative to help people to think in terms of the team, to value it and to put an effort into making it a reality. This is a particular responsibility for social work, given this function of team coordination.

Link person. For this function (2), besides the general we will need to know the specific: what each person is contributing in this instance, their aims and means. As professionals we sometimes forget that what is routine to us is a frightening unknown to sufferers and their families. What will happen in hospital, what will happen when people are discharged, medication and its effects and side-effects and a plethora of other questions are likely to be thrown at the social worker, reflecting people's uncertainty and anxiety, but also their wish to support what is being done by the team. We need to be clear about each contribution if we are to help effectively. There will be times, obviously, when we will have to say 'I don't know, but I will find out and let you know.' People are reasonable: they do not expect us to know everything off the cuff.

Linking clients with resource systems. Function (3) reminds us that what the clinical team contributes is limited. As we saw earlier, a range of practical and social resources, in addition to the professional contribution, are essential to the well-being of the sufferer. Where these resource systems do not exist, all the professionals can offer is rather poor and expensive substitutes. The best of, say, residential care cannot really replace home and family. While at any one point in time some contributions may be more significant than others, we are ultimately interdependent and it is important that the professionals remember this. Carers will sometimes complain resentfully that the professionals are 'client-focused', do not see them as significant colleagues and, by inference, disparage what they are doing. Myopia about others' contributions can lead professionals into an inflated sense of their own significance. Reinforced by their specialised knowledge and powerful social position, they can adopt a patronising attitude, reduce carers to adjuncts and make sufferers feel little more than pawns. Such attitudes have helped produce the user movement (Chamberlin, 1988; Brandon, 1991) which is basically a demand for respect: a collective expression that consumers (sufferers, families and carers) must be taken seriously or we will lose them as resources with all the consequences for what we are trying to achieve.

Much of what was written in Chapter 4, axiom 4, and around axiom 1 in this chapter has a clear relevance to this function of linking, and needs no further elaboration here. Social work has always had at its core a concern for the whole person. From this stems our functions of team coordination, linking the team with the people we serve, and linking people with other resources. To discharge these functions we need to know what the treatment programme is.

Seeing that the treatment programme is implemented and reviewed

It was Drake's prayer that recognised it was not the beginning but the continuing of an enterprise which led to a successful outcome. Social work with psychosis sufferers, their families and carers can be a lengthy business. In some instances (such as the dementias) success may be limited to preventing deterioration, arresting the speed of it, or ensuring as far as possible that the quality of life is maximised in the face of progressive decline. These are still very worthwhile outcomes, but very much more can be done in other instances – at best returning sufferers and their families to full recovery. The psychoses still carry an image of hopelessness since we cannot (as yet) cure the conditions, only control the symptoms to a degree while the illness takes its course; social work intervention can be seen as merely a protracted palliative. They are the types of 'cases' which, according to Rees (1978), social workers and their employers find the least attractive. One of the primary motivations of my teaching over the years (and of this book) has been to try to show that social work can make a fundamental difference to the quality of life of sufferers, families and carers. A conviction that we have much to offer is the essence of commitment: we will continue to do little until we acknowledge how much we can do. Securing the implementation of programmes is highly pertinent in this regard.

It is also a derivative of the functions of team 'secretary', team/ home link and link with other resources, formal (public) and informal (network). While the functions remain, the way they are discharged can change over time, reflecting technological and policy developments. In my early practice, for example, it was a primary expectation of social workers that they would see the patient 'kept on taking the tablets'. As most mental welfare officers were ex-nurses they knew about medication. With the development of community psychiatric nursing, medication is now much more a matter for them. though it is still important for social workers to remember that failure to maintain medication remains one of the primary causes of relapse.

Programme implementation has three elements: establishing contacts, reporting back and reviews:

- *Establishing contacts.* The crucial aspect of implementation is seeing that the sufferer takes up, establishes and sustains the various contacts the programme prompts. While this is easily said, it can be a complex social work task. There can be a good deal of resistance to deal with before even a contact is made and from various sources – sufferer, family and other carers and even those 'receiving' the sufferer. It is important to ease this if it is not to quietly poison the subsequent engagement. Sustaining people in contacts and engagements can make the difference between persistence and giving up. Ironing out the practical problems (transport, money) and the emotive (misunderstandings, irritations) will be tangible activities in a process that will rely heavily on intangibles such as support and encouragement – especially when the going is hard or progress comes to an apparent halt. Here I am not just thinking of work with the ill person and the family, but all the carers and resource systems: helping them to understand and persist when they get fed up, angry and disappointed by the attitudes, demands or lack of response in the people they are trying to assist. Interpretation *to* the team can be as much a function for the social worker as interpretation *of* the team, and at times may border on advocacy even with colleagues.

- *Reporting back.* All through there is the responsibility for the social worker to report back to the clinical team on the effectiveness (or otherwise) of the different contributions as s/he sees them reflected during contacts with the home situation. This will not happen so much now, but I can recall clients on medication who did not see their GP for many months, collecting repeat prescriptions via the practice receptionist. They would report that their symptoms were beginning to recur, or that they felt they were becoming zombies. Either way, their medication needed review. In an unavoidably brief out-patient appointment with the consultant psychiatrist (or one of his team), a patient with depression could report that 'everything was fine' when to my knowledge this was not so. 'I didn't want to go into my troubles when he was so busy with people a lot worse than me' may have been meant kindly, but it really did not help anyone. At the day centre, good progress was apparently being made, but at home no improvement in a client's social skills was reported: the translation from one situation to the other was not being made for some reason or other. In the day hospital the patient was as disruptive as ever, but people were gratified by the positive changes they had seen at home, so something was occurring.

  In these examples, the need for feedback is obvious enough. Doing it is not always that easy, especially if the process could imply a criticism of others' practice. This is where relationships and trust between the various members of the team are so important. Nor is the traffic one way: other team members will pick up and need to reflect back on perceptions of the social worker and his/her practice effectiveness.

- *Team reviews.* Regular team reviews are vital. Depending on what is happening, the time may have arrived for another look at the assessment to see whether the team have been over- or underestimating capacity. If the aims look realistic, the means may not be the most useful and progress could perhaps be resumed by a change. With certain goals achieved, now may be the time to move the programme along and introduce new elements to attain further objectives. May be the final goals have been realised and it is time to consolidate and terminate. We must avoid getting bogged down in a chronic situation where people are just going through the

motions and habit has taken over from thought. As team facil-
itator it is the social worker's responsibility to see this does not
happen. Sufferer and family are obviously essential to the
review process and must be incorporated in discussion and
decision-making. Without their full participation, little will work
effectively.

6

Working for the Sufferer: The Environment

This chapter is again built around two axioms with wide ramifications. The first addresses the mentally ill person's environment, and the second his/her place within it.

Axiom I: secure an appropriate environment

The appropriate environment is simply that which best meets the needs of sufferers at that time and promotes their well-being without prejudicing their future. The significance of the environment in mental illness is irrefutable at a range of levels. At the societal level, the connections with poverty, unemployment, poor housing, homelessness and social isolation have been amply demonstrated (Brown and Harris, 1979; Townsend, Davidson and Whitehead, 1988; Barham and Hayward, 1991). Even allowing for slippage down the social scale that illness of any sort can bring, especially chronic illness, there is still more 'cause' in social conditions than 'effect' of illness in the connection between mental illness and deprivation. Social work's concern for social change is as much to do with the primary prevention of mental illness as child abuse or crime, though it rarely gets the attention these other issues receive. Mental health social work may be specialised, but in this regard it is as generalist as any other areas of practice.

It is also generalist in that people with a mental illness have the universal human needs for a sufficient income, a decent place to live, a supportive social life and a dignified place in society. In striving for these we are likely to be up against overt and covert prejudice which denies full citizenship to mentally ill people, with the covert the more difficult to deal with. Overtly, people with a history of mental illness are now protected to a degree under the provisions of the

Disablement Discrimination Act 1995 – predominantly in the sphere of employment; but there are many other disadvantages that accrue: the inappropriate rigidity of the social security rules, the deleterious factors in commercial insurance policies, the health, justice and other formal systems which subtly discount users, putting difficulties in their way, according them a low priority, giving them a poorer service and generally discounting them. Even more difficult to deal with are the many informal covert expressions which result in mentally ill people being victimised, ostracised, or regarded with suspicion, effectively disbarring them from ordinary social life. There has been progress in these spheres but there is still a way to go as MIND's Respect campaign indicated (Reed and Baker, 1996). The issues are being tackled from both ends, as it were, with campaigning organisations tackling the media especially: countering negative imagery (Philo and Henderson, 1993), getting across the realities of illness, its effects and its treatment requirements. At the local level, individuals and groups are demonstrating that people with a mental illness are capable citizens, have a social contribution to make through the arts, self-help groups, services to fellow sufferers and services to the general public such as information centres and help lines. Again, it was enlightening to observe how many applications for funding to the MIND Millenium Awards panel were in this sphere.

At the individual level, the mental health social worker will be as concerned as any colleague with the basics of living and similarly engaged with the range of agencies involved with finance, accommodation, employment, recreation and self-development. The tasks and skills employed will be the same as for any other client group but with a particular place for educative work, given the persisting ignorance and prejudice about mental illnesses, and a special need of advocacy (discussed in more detail later) since some sufferers will have a limited capacity to represent themselves. A secure basic living situation is as essential for any further work with mentally ill people as it is for any other client.

Special factors

Before looking at environmental factors in psychosis more generally, three points should be made, each specific to one of the psychoses:

1. *Dementia*. One of the crucial losses in dementia is the ability to
    make new memories. The logical outcome of this is to try to
    change as little as possible in the environment or the patterns of
    life it generates. Change involves new learning and so plays
    straight into the sufferer's area of weakness. When an elderly
    confused person is admitted to residential care, the common report
    is that the confusion gets markedly worse. We need to try to stab-
    ilise people in their familiar surroundings; that is, in that setting
    where the memory they have can best be utilised.
2. *Depression*. As mentioned earlier, many people with an endoge-
    nous depression will look for explanations for the way they feel in
    their environment – house, neighbourhood, job, spouse – and
    seek a cure by changing them. Far from helping, they are only
    alienating the people in their support systems, dragged through
    the consequences of illness-induced perceptions to no avail. As a
    general rule, the middle of a depression is not the place from which
    major life decisions should be taken.
3. *Schizophrenia*. Here the concern is the so-called EE factor: the
    level of expressed emotion in the sufferer's environment. The
    work of Brown, Birley and Wing (1972) and Vaughan and Leff
    (1976) identified the EE level as the key, together with stress-
    ful life events, to understanding relapse and readmission rates.
    Put simply, if the EE level is too high (involving intensive feel-
    ings) the sufferer becomes overstimulated and develops a
    florid recurrence of the illness. The most damaging EE is hostil-
    ity, but an anxious smothering, overprotective concern can be
    almost equally disturbing. At the same time, understimulation
    can lead to boredom, apathy, a loss of volition and a slide
    towards catatonia. The work of Taylor, Huxley and Johnson
    (1984) seems to suggest that the ideal balance would be lim-
    ited intimate relationships (limited, that is, by number and
    amount of time spent in them), but a range of social contacts
    involving amiable but relatively superficial relationships.

With these particular elements in mind, the general social work task
regarding the sufferer's environment would be (a) to assess the current
environment in the light of the needs of the sufferer to determine
whether those needs are being met; (b) to assess whether unmet
needs might be met by modifications to the existing environment; or

(c) whether to meet them requires a radical shift to an alternative environment. The process would apply whether the aims were arrestive (trying to preserve what the sufferer has and make the most of it) or promotional (fostering recovery).

Assessing the current environment

In examining the environment to determine whether to intervene and if so where, when and how, there would be (in the light of what has been argued up to now) six factors to consider, some of which might be more significant than others in particular circumstances:

1. *Supervision*. Are there people around (or to be found) who can help to ensure that the sufferer comes to no harm, does not harm others and can see that medical and other programmes are carried through?
2. *Stimulation*. Are the levels too high or too low; what is the nature of it; where does it originate; is it helping or hindering the well-being of the ill person?
3. *Learning*. What does the ill person need to develop in the way of technical, social and living skills, and does the current environment provide the necessary opportunities? Might it even be teaching the wrong things, such as 'learned helplessness'?
4. *Expectations*. What expectations are being communicated to the sufferer and are they pitched too high, inviting failure, or too low, resulting in underachievement?
5. *Contribution*. In what ways is the sufferer able to contribute to others? Has s/he opportunities to develop a positive self-worth and a valued place in a social group?
6. *Care*. Are there people around who can offer the care, support, continuity, security, practical services and a sense of belonging we all need for a fundamental sense of well-being? Do the people around need help to sustain what they are doing?

The answers to these should provide some clear indicators of where we need to focus our efforts.

Modifying the existing environment

Even in ordinary life, radical changes of environment have elements
of crisis and risk, even where we have looked forward to them. Studies
have shown how stressful moving house can be, or even just getting
away on holiday. In social work with ill people we should surely start
from the premise that people stay where they are unless there are very
strong reasons for considering a move. Depending on the needs,
and assuming people are in their own homes, it seems to me that
environmental modifications can be of three kinds:

1. *What can be brought in to meet needs.* The potential range of services
   and skills is wide: home helps, family aides, meals on wheels,
   community psychiatric nursing, occupational therapy, GP, chiro-
   podist, minister of religion, voluntary visitor, sitter, peripatetic
   hairdresser, mobile shop and so on. The constraints will be what is
   available and what the sufferer and/or their families will allow in.
   To respect the latter is significant if we believe in the principle and
   efficacy of self-determination. In our own homes, self-determination
   is usually maximised (another reason for helping people to stay
   in them); we can largely decide who crosses our boundaries or
   not. In a residential 'home' it is predominantly the staff who have
   this power, however benignly exercised. When client or family
   says 'no', a social worker may be irritated, especially if they have
   worked hard to secure a resource they are sure would be of benefit;
   but at least the self-assertion of a denial has a value. There may
   be difficulties to be sorted out where one person is saying 'yes'
   but someone else is saying 'no'.
2. *What we can get the sufferer out to.* Day centres, clubs, out-patient
   appointments, educational or recreational centres; outings,
   shopping, cafes, pubs; voluntary work, part- or full-time work, work
   experience or work training, and so on – the list is again wide, the
   constraints again availability and acceptability. The latter may be
   harder to gain since it means people leaving their own territory
   for someone else's – rather more fraught.
       For both 'ins' and 'outs' there will be the need for thought, dis-
   cussion, planning, preparation, introduction and sustaining –
   activities we have already noted in connection with programme
   implementation, since this is part of it. Activities of this kind are
   a regular feature of social work and need no elaboration here.

3. *Addressing attitudes, feelings and interactions operating detri-mentally in the sufferer's environment*. Obviously the main focus will be upon working with the significant people in that envir-onment, usually members of the family. We could be dealing with a mixture of longstanding family feelings, relationships and dynamics, with all their positives, negatives and ambival-ences, together with the specific reactions of family members to the illness and the coping strategies that have been adopted to deal with those reactions. Out of this mix, many families will manage well and constructively; but others may resort to stra-tegies that are counterproductive in the longer run. We will be looking at some of these matters in more detail in Chapter 7, but briefly, here, families may hide sufferers away, fearful of the social consequences for the sufferer and themselves; or they may isolate the ill person and carry on with their lives as though s/he did not exist. They may become totally absorbed in the care of the sufferer, the pivot around which their lives revolve. The ill member may become the focus of hostility, be overprotected out of a sense of guilt, or looked after out of a sense of duty but with a barely hidden resentment at the loss of 'other things I might be doing with my life'. The situation may be further complicated because the strategies adopted by individual members of the family are incompatible, creating tensions between them and inconsistencies in approach to their ill member, making matters yet more difficult for him/her. One may be saying 'He's been ill: he needs to take it easy until he's really well again', while another suggests 'You're spoiling him. 'He's just bone idle and needs to get up off his bottom and do some work.'

There is ample scope here for the use of social work counselling skills, whether with individuals, family sub-systems or the family system as a whole. If counselling is not feasible for any reason, then there may be scope for other techniques such as behaviour modification to help the family towards less dysfunctional ways of handling matters. Sometimes we shall have to acknowledge that the changes we seek are not possible; certain factors are immut-able and we shall have to find ways round them by other means.

Besides the family there may be a range of people whose attitudes are crucial to the programme of meeting needs: neighbours, employers, the corner shopkeeper, and the many others who make up the network on which we rely for our social survival. There may be little work to be done with them except perhaps some education to shift attitudes, previously based upon mythology and misconception, towards greater realism. Even if we do not change attitudes generally, people may be prepared to make exceptions for a particular individual ('He's different'). They may help if they are given the chance to ventilate their misgivings and are assured that someone is readily available to 'pick up the pieces' should something go awry. Now and again we will be up against a person or group who cannot be persuaded, perhaps because of some irrationality to which we have no access. Anyone who has been involved in trying to open a hostel for people recovering from a mental illness in a residential district is likely to know this phenomenon.

In this environmental work people are not clients in the usual sense of that word. The professional focus and remit relate to the sufferer and, though this could conceivably take us some way into any difficulties people may have, the effect on interactions with the sufferer remains our mandate, not the difficulties *per se*. People are colleagues, not clients, with particular roles, functions and tasks to contribute. Our aim is to help them to bring their contribution to bear constructively for the benefit of the ill person. The professional is trained to make a contribution of a specific kind; the layman may need some help with what is often a more diffuse kind of involvement. While not all lay people will welcome help, many are looking for it and feel let down by the professionals if they do not get it. It is important we recognise how we are thinking of people in the environment and how this might be colouring our approach to them.

There is a possible trap here. The majority of social work practice methods derive from direct work with clients. This leaves us exposed to two risks: first, that we do not recognise that skills developed in direct work are transferable and can be used in indirect work (with non-clients, if you like), albeit to different ends. Our indirect work is less effective as a consequence. Second, because we are using the skills we can make the assumption that the people we are dealing with are clients and treat them as such, much to their resentment – and with a similarly detrimental effect on our work.

Alternative environments

If we cannot modify the existing environment to meet sufferers' current and emergent needs, then we may eventually be obliged to consider a move to an environment where they could be met more effectively, especially if the needs were urgent and salient. Some of these alternative environments could be ones that anyone might use (lodgings, a bed-sitter and so on), but many will be specially constructed to meet needs that cannot be met in customary environments: hospitals would be the obvious example. Constructed environments are typically based on the premise that people stay for only a limited time while a certain range of needs are met, and then move on elsewhere. The 'elsewheres' need to exist, however, otherwise the original premise is subverted and that environment forced to perform a task for which it was never intended. Hospital becomes home, a function for which it is not designed, because there is no other home for people to move to. (Alternatively, if it is true to its function, a hospital discharges people into the street once their treatment is complete.)

We might identify the potential alternative environments as:

- hospital,
- hostel (staffed full-time),
- group living/sheltered housing (partly staffed),
- independent living with support (regular social work and/or other inputs),
- independent living with support as requested, or
- interdependent living: shared on a family or quasi-family basis, with support, if any, only as requested.

'Fostering' (adult placement schemes) could also be added to this list; where it would fit in would depend on the type. For some very dependent people it would amount to residential care, for others it would equate to hostel care, supported living or quasi-family living.

These environments have been listed as a kind of progression, the professional team gradually withdrawing as a recovering sufferer is able to take increasing responsibility for him/herself and grows in ability to relate successfully to others. (In reverse order the list can also be thought of as a regression as a condition deteriorates.) This may not be the most helpful way of regarding them in practice; they should be seen rather as a range of facilities to be drawn upon as necessary. Very few people progress (or regress) by such routes: most

people with an acute illness go straight to hospital and when they
recover go straight home.

Clearly, if a person is acutely ill and in urgent need of medical and
nursing care more or less on a 24 hours a day basis, then hospital is
the appropriate environment. When these conditions do not apply,
hospital is inappropriate – or worse, given all we now know about the
effects of institutionalisation. We need as much drive to get people
out of hospital as we sometimes invest in getting them in. The same
approach goes for other environments: hostels can be as institution-
alising as hospitals; sheltered housing can foster dependency; support systems become an unnecessary crutch. In this sense we ought
to view anything but unsupported interdependent living as a temporary expedient. It is acknowledged that this will not hold in all circumstances, such as where the condition is typically deteriorating, as in
dementia, or where the sufferer's recovery is realistically only partial
and a degree of dependency inevitably remains. The attitude of mind
is important, nevertheless.

Expectations and procedures

One of the practical problems many approved social workers
must currently face is how to handle what I might term 'sub-acute'
situations: the person is not really ill enough for hospital but needs
some sort of asylum for a while; but the only available asylum is the
hospital – a catch-22. If a hostel were appropriate and available
there could still be hurdles. From experience I can think of two in
particular: attitudes and procedures:

1. *The set of expectations around the function of the hostel.* During
    my practice years, I was involved with a local authority hostel ori-
    ginally set up to offer a six-month rehabilitation programme for
    long-term patients discharged from hospital. When I knew it, the
    patients who could benefit from such a programme had largely
    been through it and the hostel was endeavouring to help much
    more damaged people, more disabled by illness, the length of time
    they had been in hospital, or both. The rehabilitation possible
    would take a good deal longer than six months. The professional
    staff had recognised the change of function, but found they had
    to defend what they were doing to the local authority elected

members whose original expectations remained. When a resident had stayed for more than six months they wanted to know why. Their attitude was reinforced by the suspicion that the professionals had 'sold them a pup': that they were trying to push onto the local authority (and its council-tax payers) the long-term care of mentally ill people which they regarded as a Health Service responsibility. In cases such as this the financial background arrangements will have a symbolic as well as a practical dimension.

This is an illustration of the way in which demands change, but it takes time for us to catch up with them and reflect them in the provisions we make. There is a particular temptation when we have made a considerable investment in bricks and mortar to keep it going: to fill the beds/places as evidence of demand and keep per capita costs down to demonstrate efficiency and safeguard jobs. We become pressurised to refer people even though the facility is really not suitable for them.

2. *The admission procedures.* To go back to my example, the hostel envisaged a one-way route – in from hospital and out to the community – and designed its admission procedures accordingly. Applications were considered by a small committee and, of the documentation required, the psychiatrist's report was the most significant. This system was not well-suited to coping with relatively short-notice admissions from the community. It also meant that all residents had to become a consultant psychiatrist's patient, in effect, whether they needed or wanted to do so. In such situations it becomes ever more important to see that procedures facilitate access to resources rather than set up barriers to them, although obviously any facility has the right to select who crosses its boundaries in the light of its purposes and resources. Too often, I feel, sufferers and their difficulties have to be crunched into the right shape (to fit definitions) at the right time (as resources become available) on the right form (to satisfy the bureaucracy). I doubt if sufferers or their families see these tendencies as a caring way of meeting their needs.

Planning moves to alternative environments

Apart from hospitals, we are now beginning to develop alternative community facilities to cope with emergency and short-notice short-term admissions where asylum rather than treatment is the principal need. My main concern here, though, are moves which can be set up over time, ideally with the accompanying consideration, selection, matching, preparation, introduction and sustaining processes involving all the parties concerned. Moves which are hurried, pushed or unsupported are likely to break down sooner or later.

However carefully prepared, all moves involve risk (Ramon, 1988). They make demands in anticipation of the move (coping with the apprehension generated even if specific preparational factors are not always involved), and demands for adaptation after the move into a new way of life. These apply to the mover and the people already in the new environment. There will be differences, too, for the people the mover has left behind, which will also call for adjustment. I remember a client who developed a reactive depression when, after caring for a disabled husband for many years, she finally had to relinquish him to hospital care.

There can be a natural reluctance to exchange the 'devil we know' for one we do not; and even in an overall damaging situation there can be some positive elements that may be missed subsequently – objects, places, occupations and people; whether family, friends or staff. Even after the most welcome of shifts there may be some grief work to be done before the new opportunities can be fully taken up. Reluctant shifts will make the grief work harder. This will be especially true of people surrendering their homes and entering residential care, probably for the remainder of their lives. In moving people there are two temptations to be resisted:

1. Under pressure of an unhappy situation, we may grasp at any alternative base that happens to be available, suitable or not. We then proceed to 'sell' the facility to the sufferer, lauding the advantages and ignoring the snags. We 'sell' the sufferer to the facility, presenting him/her as the ideal resident/tenant/lodger. This is a clear recipe for disaster: the wrong place and a set of totally unrealistic expectations. Better to try to sustain even an unhappy situation until a really appropriate alternative environment is to be found.
2. It is too easy for the worker, under pressure, to let go once the physical shift has been accomplished, to get on with 'more urgent' tasks. Promises, specific or implied, of continued contact get buried by more clamant demands. The follow-through needs to be sustained: the disappearing social worker is too common a phenomenon.

In an urgent situation, where the sufferer, family or others are demanding a shift, the initial social work task is to decide whether to accede to this pressure or not. Either way there will be volatility to work with. In non-urgent situations, the volition may well be the worker's, generated by his/her perceptions of the advantages of a move. In these circumstances, the first task may well be to generate volition in others, with the response of the sufferer being the most crucial. While some will welcome the prospect of a move, others will have apprehensions that will need to be dealt with about, say, moving out of hospital to a hostel or from a hostel into their own accommodation. Others will say 'no' and it can be distressing to stand by while someone becomes further institutionalised or continues to be exploited. We may toy with the idea of a guardianship order or wish we had a community treatment order available to us with control over where the sufferer resides: something between the sledgehammer of a compulsory admission to hospital and the helplessness of having nothing to safeguard a sufferer's well-being as we see it.

I am not convinced an order would be helpful in this kind of move. More than anything, a successful 'transplant' is going to depend on the positive motivation of the sufferer. If they are pushed into moving by the use of orders, resistance (overt or covert) is likely to sabotage the shift. A holding operation to protect the sufferer from severe immediate damage is the best we might get out of such an order. What will matter is the skill of the worker and the degree of trust between him/her and the client. A move of base can be a stringent test of the quality of our work, which may be one reason why we often approach the task guardedly and are sometimes tempted to wish for statutory power to help us out. The real beneficiary of orders should be the client, since an order should give him/her a lien on both the social worker and the agency to provide the services and resources s/he needs. We should think less of the powers orders give us and more of the obligations they put us under, perhaps.

Complicating factors in planning moves

There are four further factors which complicate shifts of environment:

1. A deterrent to getting involved with moves may be our qualms about *the quality of alternative base we are contemplating using.* While the physical qualities may be comparatively obvious, the

quality of the relationships and social processes that go with them are harder to gauge. Nor are they constant: what we knew of them some time ago may not be true of them now. Keeping in touch becomes a necessity.

2. The obverse of our concern about the quality of the base is our guilt, sometimes, about *what we are asking the base to take on*, knowing the kind of difficulties the sufferer can present. It has already been suggested that 'selling' someone is not a good idea. Staff at the new environment will quickly find out for themselves anyway and subsequent approaches will be regarded with suspicion, to the detriment of others we are trying to help.

3. Since we set up domiciliary and community-based services there has been a *subtle tension between field-based workers and providers of alternative environments*. The field operators worry about how they would manage at times if there were no alternatives available to them, and so feel beholden. The alternative environment providers often depend on referrals from field practitioners and so feel they have to keep on good terms or their supply will dry up and they will be out of a job or business. Perceived power or vulnerability can tempt us into game-playing to suit our own interests rather than those of our clients.

4. The above factors can be yet further complicated by the *financial factors*. Who pays for what in the field of health/rehabilitation/ care services has always been rather hazy. If there has been a tendency in recent years it would seem to be that central government, apprehensive of rising budgetary implications (and especially that of the long-term care of elderly people) has shuffled increasing responsibility on to local authorities where it can. In response to the constraints facing them, local authorities have passed the squeeze to others in two principal ways:

    (a) by contracting out their services and then limiting the fees they pay – whether to commercial, non-profit making or voluntary organisations. This obviously effects the quality of such services, if not the very existence of them.
    (b) by levying charges on users for services that were previously free of charge.

    The variations in the financial situations of authorities, their priorities and their different charging policies have given rise to complaints of 'post-code' inequalities in local authority services as well as the NHS. The complications of anomalies between national social security regulations and local assessment systems can also be significant at times when thinking of shifts of environment. Many groups remain critical of the provisions of the NHS & Social Care legislation 2001 which do little to remedy these matters While the nursing functions in social care are to be free of cost, personal care (often difficult to distinguish from nursing) and 'hotel' care remain chargeable – though remaining free in hospitals.

The policy principle that people should remain in/return to their own homes since this is overwhelmingly what they wish, seems right. It is also conveniently cheaper in some people's view, though, as previously mentioned, whether this is really so is dubious. This suggests there will be pressures against shifts to alternative environments unless they can be shown to be definitely economic, rehabilitative or absolutely inevitable. On the other hand, a shortfall in the provision of primary care can lead to unwanted and unnecessary residential care – for example the bed blocking in the NHS resulting from the shortfall in Social Services provision. This may mean financial savings to the primary care services when costs are thus transferred to other systems or the individual or their family if they have the income or assets. At least if people move and take an adequate budget with them it should enable sufferers or their advocates to exercise choice – an important element in making a transfer successfully. The corollary, an obliged 'Hobson's choice' move, can prickle with difficulties.

The policy and practice environment in which the social worker operates will, as always, have a profound influence on what s/he is able to achieve in efforts to implement this axiom – to secure the appropriate environment for the sufferer. Hence our professional concern to try to influence that policy to promote good practice and benefit our clients. The discussion of this axiom concludes with three points:

1. Resistance to movement of base can come from other than the person with a mental illness. Some families may resist a movement 'out': perhaps because they see such a move being interpreted by others as a slur on their ability or willingness to care for one of their own. More profoundly, if rarely, taking the sufferer out

might be dysfunctional for them if in the process they lose either their scapegoat or their rationale for staying together. The presence of the ill member may be a defence against issues too painful for them to look at. Very occasionally resistance can come from the professional people supposed to be assisting the sufferer to move on. From practice I recall a senior member of staff being quite irritated when it was suggested we try to discharge from hospital the patient who had been a *de facto* daily help for a good many years. I have also known short-handed nursing staff reluctant to consider the discharge of long-stay patients who were valuable to them in running the ward: who had become, in effect, unpaid nurse auxiliaries.

Obviously, too, there can be resistances to move 'in': a family is happy with the way things are and does not want this disturbed by any intrusion; doctors, nursing staff, hostel staff and others may resist admitting sufferers they see as demanding or troublesome. The aggressive, uncooperative stirrer or the cantankerous, incontinent wanderer are not particularly welcome, especially when staff are already under pressure. A lot of work may be needed before a proposed move can begin – in or out.

2. In the 'shifting of base' area of mental health practice there is much to be learned from child-care practice. On the negative side, we should heed the devastating effects of constantly moving people and in the process killing off what remaining contacts they had with their families. It is professionally a disgrace that youngsters leaving care form such a high proportion of the rootless in our city centres; and it is an equal shame that so many homeless people are ex-psychiatric patients. Positively, the fostering, adoption and residential care of children have produced a literature of good practice that with little modification could provide us with models of real value in the mental health sphere.

3. The pressures, more especially in hospitals, to clear beds to accommodate people on the waiting list or to facilitate the closure of wards, present social workers with both practical problems and moral dilemmas. If the hospital has perforce become home for the past 30 years, the ethics of pushing out a patient who wants to stay are dubious to say the least. It is also questionable to move a patient into a makeshift alternative, with every risk of a swift re-admission. The 'revolving door' is given another twist. The closure phenomenon is also known in the community

care sector where the commercial failure of homes is a real threat. To preserve one's professional integrity in such circumstances, the backing of agency, colleagues or both may become an essential. Membership of a professional social work organisation can be a vital matter for every practitioner.

Axiom II: secure a routine

Securing the appropriate environment is one half of an equation: the other is to establish the place of the sufferer within it. It is suggested that the best way to do this is by securing a satisfactory and satisfying routine for him/her in that environment.

The importance of routines

There are very few of us who do not have a basic rhythm to our lives. We get up, wash, dress, eat, go out to work/school, lunch, back to work, come home, have a meal, spend the evening, go to bed. Even the way we spend our 'free' time develops patterns: regular occasions for sport, evening classes, going out with friends, washing hair, watching favourite television programmes and so on. Weekends will be regularised with shopping, gardening, DIY, visiting relatives, staying up on Saturday evening, lying in reading the papers on Sunday morning or going to church. We do not realise how patterned our lives are until something happens to disrupt our day-to-day living. Some of these events are ordinary life stages such as leaving school, getting a job, getting married, parenthood, grandparenthood, retirement. Some are traumas: redundancy, bereavement, a stroke, a crippling accident, divorce. Either type will involve us, as individuals and families, in putting together new patterns which will hopefully provide us with sufficient satisfaction, from physical survival to self-realisation. Not all changes are sudden ones; some will involve a slow adaptation over the years: parents accommodating to their children as they grow up or, as we get older, acknowledging we cannot always manage what we once accomplished.

For the most part, people cope with the changes that life events, trauma or adaptation require with the support of their informal social networks. It is where people do not find sufficiently satisfying patterns that the formal systems may come into play. An unhappy couple seek a divorce, a bereaved person develops a reactive depression, stress provokes acute anxiety or a resort to drugs or alcohol. Such reactions will bring people to the notice of the professionals.

Patterns, then, are important since they routinely contribute to the satisfaction of needs, give our lives stability and predictability, and are also significant as a means of economising effort. We do not have to think things through afresh every time; routines carry us along without the need to constantly initiate. Many decisions come almost ready-made; we do not have to make them over and over again, and our energies then can go elsewhere. Yet reconstructing patterns involves real effort at a time when people can be at a low ebb. If their experiments with change meet with disappointment and failure, a further burden is added.

Routines and mental illness

Mental illness, whether the onset is gradual or relatively sudden, is going to disrupt patterns; both the sufferer's and their family's. They are going to need help to sustain some of the patterns they had and to rebuild others constructively. It will not be easy. The excited schizophrenia sufferer will largely disrupt routines, while a lethargic phase of the illness may mean only marginally less of an upheaval. A person with depression finds everything an effort; the dementia sufferer is constantly side-tracking, given their shaky hold on the here and now.

Securing a routine is closely linked to what has already been written about helping a sufferer to maintain contact with reality, promoting their self-management skills, establishing a network, developing and sustaining treatment programmes and creating an appropriate environment. The routine puts these elements together into a meaningful, day-to-day structure. It will be the social worker's task to help identify the elements needed, to negotiate their practical form, and to support and sustain their implementation. As a basis, we need to recognise certain principles which should underlie our dealings with any client, ill or not. Patterns should (a) leave people with a manageable degree of responsibility, recognising they are adults and respecting their dignity; (b) give them a manageable degree of self-direction, affording them the maximum room to make their own choices; and (c) leave them with the maximum opportunity for self-fulfilment consistent with the rights of others.

If routines are the principled and practical implementation of planning, certain elements will need to be in place within them. Broadly these are three:

1. The opportunity for the person with the mental illness to maintain or develop, as necessary, technical skills required for daily living.
2. Social relationships of a sufficient range and balance of intensity to provide stimulus, but not to overstimulate; the opportunity to acquire or maintain social skills; and the chance to contribute on a reciprocal basis in dignifying social interaction.
3. A network, with its functions of 'keeping an eye', support and contribution; backed up to see that it is not overstretched.

As these elements have been discussed earlier, they are only identified to make the connection with establishing routines. However, four aspects of pattern-building need to be explored further: the use of pressure to maintain patterns; the use of structured social situations; accommodating symptomatology and structuring opportunity.

- *The use of pressure to maintain patterns.* The likeliest perpetual question emerging from family and network will be how much pressure to use to keep patterns going. Parents will want to know whether their son suffering from schizophrenia should be made to get up at a reasonable hour in the morning rather than allowed to lie in bed until lunchtime. The spouse of a depressed person will be wondering how far to lean on a partner to get him/her to work, shop, garden, cook, even to dress presentably. The children of an elderly parent with dementia will worry over just how many times they have to remind him/her to do this, that or the other. Each of these scenarios has two basic risks:

  (1) To seem to be constantly nagging the sufferer will antagonise him/her and make the maintenance of routines even more difficult. Matters may be complicated if this pressurising function fits uneasily with significant earlier roles and relationships. It can be hard for 'children' to 'parent' their own mother or father and for a parent to accept this. It will be far from easy for a spouse to become more directive when the

past pattern has been to share decisions, or even for them to
be the more submissive, while their partner may resent being
'pushed around'. Parents who have let their children grow
into independence can find it hard to go back to partly controlling them again; their 'child' may not welcome it either.

(2)   The risk of creating dependency by becoming the ill person's
director, in effect. In this sense, oddly, the antagonism,
resentment, tension and resistance which might seem a threat
to relationships under (1) can be seen as healthy in terms of
dependency risk. 'All sweetness and light' is not an indicator
of well-being if it is achieved by mere conformity. As social
workers we are sometimes seduced into welcoming peace and
quiet since this makes things easier for us in the short term. At
bottom, we may know that good practice would suggest we
need to stir certain things up if they are not to fester under the
surface or stand in the way of further progress.

There are no ready-made answers to questions of pressure, but
judgments to be made, utilising the available experience. Again
this is an area of practice where psychiatric nursing colleagues
have much to offer.

- *The use of social structures.* In ordinary life most of our social
contacts (numerically) and much of our social satisfaction occur in
structured situations: workmates, the people we meet each morning because we use the same commuter train, local shop staff,
'regulars' at pub or club, other parents we meet collecting our
respective children from school, and so on. It is often out of these
structured situations that, if we like each other, we develop closer
ties. Those of us who have been involved in befriending schemes
will know how socially awkward it is to introduce people to each
other and (in effect) to ask them to be friends (Parish, 1998) They
may become 'matey' in style and the relationship serve useful
purposes; but rarely will it develop the spontaneity and mutuality
of a genuine friendship. We might do better to arrange patterns
which provide structured relations and enabling friendships to
emerge naturally.

- *Accommodating symptomatology.* Obviously symptoms cannot be
allowed to dominate patterns; a function of patterns is to help the
sufferer manage symptoms more effectively. It would be foolish,
though, to set up rhythms of living which run into the symptoms

head-on and so invite failure. To give examples, many people with depression experience a diurnal swing of mood: at worst in the morning, feeling better later in the day. Would there be the chance to switch their working hours, from nine to five to, say, two till ten and so enable them to keep their job rather than resign or get the sack. If their responsibilities are domestic, perhaps someone could take over getting the family up, breakfasted and on their way with a packed lunch, with the sufferer getting their main meal in the evening and so retaining a significant part of their role, contribution and dignity. Early waking is another common symptom in depression. Would it be possible, instead of lying in bed twisting and turning, for the depressed person to get up and get on with whatever can be quietly done, such as the ironing? They may go back to bed later but they would have had the satisfaction of achieving something.

The dementia sufferer may well still have a very good memory for things past. It could be more helpful to go back to the 'old fashioned' way of doing things rather than try to maintain or introduce the use of modern methods or gadgetry, however laboursaving.

Schizophrenia is such a variable condition (if it is just one) that accommodating symptoms is a complex matter. As I have said, the extremes of excitement or lethargy would be hard to contain in any routine; the priority would have to go to symptom relief. On the other hand, people who are well between florid episodes might need no particular help to establish patterns; the objective would more likely be to help them sustain the patterns they already have. Structuring in the complementary methods mentioned earlier could help to make symptoms more manageable and contribute to diminishing their effects.

Where the illness results in some permanent damage, there may be some work to do in gently persuading the sufferer into routines s/he can sustain rather than persist in aspiring to get back to, say, the employment they can now no longer manage. It is vital that routines take advantage of what people have. It is sometimes possible to capitalise on a particular aptitude; for example, with numbers or words. One patient I remember, ill enough to be in hospital long-term, was an excellent typesetter for the printing workshop. Assets need to be turned into something productive if we are to afford the sufferer a sense of achievement, the satisfaction of making a contribution and, wherever possible, the dignity of being an earner whether in open or sheltered employment.

- *Structuring opportunity*. Although we have highlighted what is seen as the importance of structured routines, it is acknowledged that these have their limitations. For the most part they carry us through the basics of living: they may or may not provide for those extra-special occasions which make life worthwhile – outings, holidays, events, and so on. People with a mental illness need these occasions as much as anyone else. Structures that can create the chance of some special occasions would be my preference.

Creating structures

Working for people with a mental illness through networking, contributing to the team, modifying the environment and establishing a routine can be difficult and time-consuming; but together with working with families, which we come to in the next chapter, the value of it is well-established (Leff *et al.*, 1982) even by such basic measures as relapse rates. There are indicators, however, that this work is not always being done. In order to develop a greater range of resources and opportunities or to make existing services more accessible to facilitate their utilisation, we sometimes create new structures of our own such as Community Mental Health Centres. Seen by some as the lynchpins of the new-style community-based service for mentally ill people, research for Good Practices in Mental Health (Patmore and Weaver, 1991) suggested they were largely catering for those people suffering from moderate emotional distress, not serious enough for hospital admission, using counselling methods principally. In effect, centres were offering a new service to troubled people whose needs had largely gone unmet in the past (except, perhaps, for a prescription for tranquillisers) – the majority of them women. Obviously this work was not to be decried; it was of great importance in itself and as a preventive measure; but it seems to have been done in preference to that with psychosis sufferers. Few centres had anything for the dementia sufferer; provision for them was largely a matter of hospital day centres, supplemented by a variable range of local authority and voluntary provision. Sufferers from schizophrenia and endogenous depression were rarely getting a better service than before, it seemed. Centres, then, would appear to risk, first, becoming a comfortable alliance of contributory staff doing what they choose, using prestigious methods such as psychotherapy with clients seen as hopeful and rewarding, and, second, financial vulnerability. To secure continued funding they may be pushed into demonstrating a high turnover to prove efficiency and value for money. Both militate against the longer-term work and the range of facilities that may be needed for psychosis sufferers. We may well have to install some systems of checks to see that community mental health services comprehensively address need and avoid the pitfalls of other services where those needing least seem to get most; those needing most get what is left over. Whatever our intentions, structures can be subverted.

Allies in working in the environment

If mental illness sufferers are going to get the services, the understanding and the respect they merit as fellow citizens, we are fundamentally addressing social attitudes. Changing them needs a combination of methods, both 'bottom-up' and 'top-down'. Basically, this book has the former orientation – practice at the individual level, but with the significance of the societal levels endemic throughout. If the responsibility for changing detrimental social attitudes had been that of the clinical team alone, I doubt we would have achieved nearly as much as has been achieved. We have had vitally important allies in the task, though it is also important to remember that they have primarily used the experience gathered at the individual level as the basis of their arguments for change. In this sense each complements the other.

Looking around, it is almost surprising how many potential allies we have, grouped, perhaps, as under:

• Organisations which set out service standards, such as the NHS Patients' Charter, (since dropped) or operate quality assurance systems. These, at least, provide some sort of leverage for complaints when sufferers experience discrimination. Even within the mental health services themselves the care planning approach is being taken further by proposals for planning to be a requisite for submissions to the new mental health tribunals when they are set up; to form part of the framework for community care and treatment orders; and for care plans to be provided compulsorily. While plans are one thing and the resources to implement them are another, nevertheless they should also afford some leverage (unless they go the way of some community care assessments, reportedly, which get tailored to fit what is available).

- Other organisations have built in means of evaluating policy and/or safeguarding standards of practice whether nationally or locally. There is a range here from Community Health Councils (provided they continue to exist; or, failing them, the proposed patients' forum and advocacy service) the Mental Health Act Commission, local authority inspectorial functions, voluntary organisations' affiliation systems, and so on. There are also appeal systems: local councillors, consumer councils and Ombudsmen, for example. Influence and powers vary very considerably but, nevertheless, these systems can be used to remedy individual or group issues. If not exactly in-built, there are times when similar functions can be exercised by an influential individual such as an MP, or ultimately through legal process in the courts.

- A wide variety of professional and other organisations whose work brings them into the mental health sphere – some professional groups almost exclusively (e.g. the Royal College of Psychiatry, the Community Psychiatric Nursing Association); others partially (e.g. the British Association of Social Workers, the Royal College of Nursing, the Royal College of General Practitioners), mental health being one among other interests. Other organisations come up against mental health matters in a particular context (e.g. trade unions in employment concerns, NACRO since many offenders have mental health problems). Some bodies have an almost ethical concern for disadvantaged groups and mentally ill people among their concerns (e.g. the Church of England Board for Social Responsibility), or they have research concerns in this field (e.g. the Mental Health Foundation). The range of organisations involved with the Mental Health Alliance is enlightening; but the range is part of its lobbying power. Many people, not least those employed in the mental health services, will contribute to the work of such organisations and/or the campaigning groups as a way of tackling the wider social issues outside the limits of their job description but part of the factors that are endemic to their practice and requiring a wider sphere of address. Perhaps, too, it is a safer and more effective way to use other organisations than their own to 'blow the whistle' should this become necessary. Despite the additional legal protection for whistle blowers, they are still vulnerable.

- Then there are the campaigning organisations (the National Schizophrenia Fellowship, the Manic Depression Fellowship, MIND, the Altzheimer's Disease Society, the Depression Alliance are examples) which gather information and opinion, process this into arguments for change, turn them into practical targets and set about attaining them, typically starting with an education programme, identifying the issues and setting out the remedies using the multiplicity of means of publicity now available from pamphlets to web sites. Marshalling the support engendered to add to their lobbying of the holders of power for change is a vitally important function, especially if the changes sought involve legislation. Not that the traffic is all one way. Campaigning organisations are often respected for their knowledge and opinion and are frequently consulted by a range of others from individuals to government departments over particular matters. This can become as influential a part of their work as lobbying in bringing about change.

- Finally, but most importantly, has been the user movement (Parsloe, 1999; Morris, 2000), which includes not just patients and ex-patients of mental health services but families and carers too, since they are also deeply effected. I term it a movement since it has only rarely spawned national organisations such as the Carers National Association or become formalised at regional or levels other than the local. Yet it has been a prime mover in creating a new climate. It seems to have operated in two main ways: through small groups of like-minded people and through participation in campaigning organisations where, in some instances, they have earned a special recognition (e.g. the Mindlink network now a constitutional part of MIND). The functions of the user movement are many but might be identified as:
  (a) *Education.* There are two main aspects to this: first, the education of the general public (including the media in particular) in the realities of mental illness, to counter the prejudicial mythology which still exists. There are many ways in which this has been tackled: pamphlets, newsletters, data banks and information lines, videos, exhibitions, books (prose and poetry) of individual experiences of illness, among them. Again, Lottery funds have helped to foster this activity.

Second has been the education of people and organisations concerned with mental health services' policies and provision, about the realities of their experience of the treatment they received/are receiving (Rose, 2001). To hear from people at the receiving end is increasingly incorporated into the formal training courses of a wide range of staff. Users can speak with a first-hand credibility on these matters that no-one else can.

(b) *Support groups.* Support has always been a function of the local groups of national organisations and users are increasingly influential in their activities; but if, again, Millennium funding is a guide, there are a rapidly growing number of small user groups, frequently exploiting modern technologies, who are developing a wide range of supportive ventures from help lines, e-mails and self-realisation activities, to alternative therapies.

(c) *Advocacy* is of particular concern to many users who have experienced the vulnerability and feelings of helplessness the processing of mentally ill people can engender: legal processes, compulsory treatment, 'voluntary' treatments that have deleterious effects, little choice of treatments, or the weight of hospital systems that allow of little individuality and seem to grind on with a heedless inevitability. Users as advocates can say to their clients with conviction 'I have been there', and set about remedying matters on ground that is familiar to them. Not that all the occasions for advocacy are directly illness-related. People with a mental illness history tend to be discounted in a range of situations as mentioned previously; they could do with some backing in these other situations, too.

(d) *Representation* is now an established facet of the user movement as advisers/consultants but increasingly as members of executive groups with a particular contribution to make.

(e) *Lobbying* for change, either through their own organisations such as Survivors Speak Out or by using existing campaigning frameworks, identifying the issues and becoming negotiators; their asset again being their credibility.

Pressures are on to establish access to advocacy as a fundamental part of mental health provision, universally available (not just for those under compulsion), and of an approved standard (Read and Wallcraft, 1995; UKAN, 1997). The various roles can be very daunting for individual users: encouragement, support and training are needed. This will be particularly true if advocates have access to the proposed Tribunals deciding detention issues.

Links with our allies are ever more important for what they can achieve in the way of change, for the services they can render our clients directly as well as indirectly, and for the opportunities to participate that they can offer our clients. There are roles, tasks and contributions that only people with a mental illness history can fulfil.

7

The Family: Responding to Needs

The pressures on families

For families, the mental illness of a member is not just a crisis, it is a prolonged crisis. Families have had a rough time for the past five decades (Mills, 1962; Rollin, 1983; NSF, 1973; Mace and Rabins, 1999; Pulling, 1987; Hatfield and Lefley, 1987; Wilcock, 1990; Deacon, 1992; Woodall, 1992; Howe, 1997). The discovery of psychotropic drugs in the 1950s meant that much more mental illness could be treated without recourse to hospital admission, or enabled earlier discharge. While this was clearly a most important breakthrough, it meant that families were now taking on much more of the primary care previously undertaken by hospital nursing staff. The anti-psychiatry movement of the 1960s, by ascribing mental illness to dysfunctional dynamics, blamed families for the illness and loaded them with even more guilt. The 1970s saw the fruition of anti-institutionalism and the start of the policy of running down the large psychiatric hospitals in favour of more localised provision. Slowly implemented at first, the policy speeded up in the later 1980s. Whatever the priorities White Papers have tried to give to health service provision for chronically ill people, it has been the acute services which have attracted the resources; chronic illness was increasingly seen as the province of community care, formalised by the Health & Social Services Act, 1993 The community services for mentally ill people failed to develop at the pace needed (Sayce, 1990; MHAC, 1992), the results of that failure emerging in surveys of homeless people and prison populations where sharp increases in the numbers and proportions of mentally ill people were being reported. Families are still overwhelmingly the principal carers, however, and are increasingly feeling the strain (CNA, 1992).

The burden has fallen on women in particular (Surma, 1991; Ungerson, 1991) exploiting their traditional caring role and adding to the evidence of the persisting inequalities between the sexes in modern society (Lewis and Meredith, 1988). Even the very limited Care Programme Approach (Dept of Health, 1990) has been inhibited for lack of resources. At least this current decade has begun more optimistically, and mental health issues are being taken seriously. The National Service Framework (Dept of Health, 1999) and legislative proposals may not embody all that the campaigning organisations might have wished, but carers and families now have the right to an assessment of their needs and, although (again) assessment is one thing and service delivery another, the prospect of some relief eventually is there (Arksey, Hepworth and Quereshi, 1998). Carers and families may have mixed feelings about proposals to replace the legal functions of the 'nearest relative' by a 'nominated person', even if they are consulted about this appointment; some may be glad to be relieved of this responsibility, others may feel angry about apparently being marginalised.

Services (or lack of them) apart, the factors which will help to determine the form and duration of the crisis for the family will be the intensity and pervasiveness of the acute illness episodes and the degree of normality achieved between them; the extent of the impairment in a persisting condition; and/or the rate of deterioration – more especially in dementia. Even where there has only been one episode of, say, depression, families may be uneasily on the watch for a long time afterwards, since no-one can say with certainty at the time whether this will be a 'one-off' or a recurrent pattern. Living with uncertainty is something families often have to get used to.

Whether it is a 'one-off' crisis, recurrent crises of episodes, or the long grind of chronicity, the family's capacity to cope and adapt is going to be severely tested. If they are to continue to care yet survive as people in their own right, they are going to need help over some time, even if the help is intermittent. Demand may be at its greatest in acute crisis, but the ideal must surely be to prevent crises wherever possible – whether occasioned by recurrence of acute illness or the collapse of care under prolonged strain. While help in a crisis is welcome, families coping with a chronic situation want more than this (Rees and Wallace, 1982). Sufferers and families appreciate social workers keeping in regular touch, whether there is a particular need or not at that moment; families do not always like to have to initiate contacts and therefore be the ones who always seem to be asking for help. They also appreciate a continuity of worker. Constant change, never knowing who is coming or who now to contact should they need to, is very off-putting. The agency can appear bureaucratic and uncaring and used only as a last resort. Families and sufferers also want a worker who 'knows his stuff' – in this instance, mental illness. S/he will have little credence otherwise. The message to agencies is clear: families want a regular service from known workers with a relevant competence. Given this foundation, delivering a service to families involves four practice axioms which will now be discussed.

Axiom I: shape intervention to the stage of adaptation reached

Stages of the process

Experience and research (for example, Hatfield and Lefley, 1987) suggests that, whichever of the psychoses is involved, the family's responses seem to have a pattern. They first notice some subtle change in the sufferer: not their usual selves, a bit out of their usual routines, some change in their habits, slightly cut off somehow. To deal with their unease, the family find some excuse for this change: the sufferer has been working hard, is physically a bit off colour; it is explicable behaviour for an adolescent, a woman entering the menopause, or for people getting on in years; they will get over it and in the meantime we will not make a fuss about it – it will only make for pointless rows. The changes do not go away, though; they get rather worse. The family now begin to worry about what might be at the bottom of it and feel they can no longer ignore it. They may take it up with the sufferer, who is likely to offer some sort of explanation, pooh-pooh their concerns or get angry; but little changes. The family turn to their usual confidants about their unease. The typical response they will get is reassurance that everything will work out; but their doubts are not put at rest. Their anxieties grow as the changes become more pronounced and they decide it is now time to get a professional opinion; customarily they turn to their GP.

The GP is faced with a difficult situation. The symptoms are still possibly rather vague to an outsider at this stage and could be ascribed to a range of physical and/or psychological factors. Though the doctor may think a beginning psychosis is one possibility, s/he is unlikely to raise this until other options have been explored, and is also going to be as reassuring as possible. Feeling more comforted, and satisfied they have 'done the right thing', the family may also feel more secure at having a prescription, the prospect of some tests, further appointments and so on: modern medicine has now got to work and we should soon find out what the matter is and get it put right; there is something we can do by seeing the sufferer cooperates in treatment.

But things may not work out; the sufferer's condition continues to deteriorate and the family resort to increasingly desperate measures to try to cope. The situation finally blows up into an acute crisis. The person with depression makes a suicide attempt; the schizophrenia sufferer locks him/herself into a bedroom and refuses to come out, or is now indulging in such bizarre and frantic activity, accompanied by weird garbled ideas, that they are impossible to contain. The dementia sufferer is found wandering the streets at night only half-dressed and convinced s/he is meeting someone long since dead.

> Mr M. aged 68, was admitted to hospital after a complaint of indecent assault by a young woman sitting in the seat next to him in a cinema. His family were deeply distressed and ashamed by the incident. They insisted the behaviour was totally out of character, but they acknowledged he had not been his usual self in a number of respects for some time.

The sufferer is now officially ill, with the panoply of the health service involved, under a consultant. Although the manifestations are behavioural, explanations (properly) will still be sought in terms of the physical. It could be some while before a mental illness diagnosis is raised and eventually confirmed. The family is likely to baulk at this diagnosis at first and cling to other explanations. Even when they acknowledge there must be something in the diagnosis after all, they may still be equivocating to themselves as well as others. The sufferer has been under a strain which has resulted in a 'nervous breakdown'. They will be in hospital for 'a rest' and will come home before very long 'cured', and their old selves again. The illness is clothed with respectable explanations, is of a temporary nature and a complete recovery is expected. It is only when such explanations are no longer tenable that the family can admit the full implications of what the diagnosis means.

Now may begin the search for causes and cures. With causes, the family might start with genetics, given the mythology (mentioned in Chapter 3) that 'madness' runs in families. A range of skeletons may be brought out of family cupboards to prove or disprove the idea or pin the blame on one side of the family or the other. Another causal area searched could be early trauma, whether illness or accident. Other ascriptions may be in the area of the sufferer's lifestyle (overwork, drinking, smoking, diet, the wrong companions or social isolation) or personality (over-conscientious, worrier, oddity) as people look for predisposing factors which would need tackling in the future if things are to be really put right and this is not to happen again. One of the commoner areas of exploration will be the way the sufferer has been treated by the family over the years, prompted by the almost inevitable guilt behind the question, 'Where did we go wrong?' This is patently a most unhappy time for most families.

For cures, the family will be heavily dependent on the medical profession, medication and the other usual forms of treatment. If these do not seem to be working, a few families might be tempted to explore what might be termed the orthodox fringe medicines such as homeopathy. In desperation a handful of families may turn to more extreme remedies, risking (as others would see it) becoming the victims of charlatans. Regrettably, though, there are times when the family has to take on the role of advocate. They, more than anyone, must know the changes in the sufferer whether due to the illness or the treatment programme. They more than anyone are likely to hear what the ill person is really feeling about themselves, their regime, and what they feel they need – whether to stop this or provide that. Motivated by their concern, families would have to find their way through the unfamiliar, powerful and pervasive mental health systems to make their representations known in the right places; to identify and justify their lobbying for changes as amateurs in a professional world; and from their knowledge over the years argue for what they consider is likely to succeed in assisting the sufferer's best recovery. There is the risk in this process that they could be disparaged or, worse, stereotyped as interfering nuisances stirring up trouble. This fear that they could be making matters worse for their ill member is a real deterrent for many families: but their failure to contribute can be just as damaging to the sufferer's interests though – a real 'catch-22' situation for them.

Should the sufferer's condition become chronic and irreversible, then a process akin to bereavement is highly likely. The shock/denial stages will have been gone through but the angry stage may now emerge ('What have I done to deserve this?'), the despair ('Everything is shattered; what is the point of anything?'), the resentment ('My life is completely messed up because of him/her') and the grief, when hope has gone, of having lost someone they loved. All the plans and hopes for the future which, whether we realise it or not, ordinarily exist in our minds, will have to be abandoned. It is a particularly difficult kind of grief to work through since the person is not physically dead. They live on, the relationship with them continues, together with the attributes and social obligations associated with it, but without the reciprocity on which it was based and the satisfactions derived from it which made it alive. It is reduced to a 'going through the motions' hollowness which can be very hard indeed to come to terms with.

The ultimate stage, the goal of the process, is acceptance. The term has overtones of resignation and there is a truth in this as far as the past person and past aspirations are concerned: as with bereavement, they have to be relinquished before life can move forward again. The acceptance of reality, though, also includes the possibilities that properly lie within it: that something can be done to improve, sustain or keep going as long as possible the quality of life for the sufferer and the family. Until the positives have been recognised, too, and are being acted upon, acceptance has not been fully reached.

Stages and responses

It is important that practitioners recognise the possible process patterns and not assume, at whichever point they become involved, that they are seeing the family as it ordinarily functions. Because they are not coping particularly well at this period in time does not mean they will be unable to cope adequately in future; or, vice versa, coping now but with problems for the future.

The process through to acceptance will not be the same for everyone in the family, since the impact of and response to the prolonged crisis will inevitably vary, depending on such factors as the degree of involvement, personality, family position and the effect of earlier family relationships. Breadwinner, home-maker, parent, sibling, adolescent, infant are going to experience matters very differently, while the reactions will be filtered through the perceptions, attitudes and feelings they have about the sufferer. Some people will get through the stages more quickly than others; some people will get held up at different parts of the process and there will be the occasional regressions. While there may be degrees of commonality in the process for the family as a whole, there will be individual differences. There may come a point when the differences become sufficiently marked for the commonality to break down. If this means those further through the process can help those still at an earlier stage, so well and good. If it leads to tension and bickering, everyone may get stuck.

Obviously the social work task is to assist the family and the individual members of it to negotiate their respective adaptive processes as constructively as possible. Direct methods would probably be the practitioner's first choice: individual counselling, family group work or using peer groups of people 'in the same boat', depending on what needed to be addressed and the most suitable means of tackling it. Not everyone finds the direct methods acceptable, however, and talking about their feelings can be hard and painful for some. They can be helped sometimes through reducing pressure by way of practical services, giving them the space to work through their feelings in their own style and time. Others may find it easier to cope if they are doing something, and some of the possible channels for activity have been indicated earlier.

This adaptive process is at its fullest and most evident where the illness is, or becomes, chronic. For other sufferers, though, the illness consists of one or recurrent episodes, either side of which they are their usual selves. In such circumstances the adaptive process may be less intense, have fewer elements, or be curtailed in duration; but it will still be there. Just one episode can leave its scars: a chronic unease about the future, with things never quite the same again. Recurrent episodes can create much more difficulty: the watchfulness and uncertainty of if/when it might happen again; the 'treading on eggshells' to try to avoid precipitating an onset; wondering whether to commit the family to future events (the theatre outing, the family wedding, the package holiday) just in case everything has to be cancelled at the last minute.

Possibly even with one episode and more probably with recurrent episodes, there will be an element of mourning for what might have been: the job or the promotion they did not get, the unborn children, the reminders when insurance companies turn down proposals, or a driving licence is queried. Acceptance remains the goal in these instances and not just those where chronic illness is involved.

> Mrs D. had abrupt eruptions of mania during which she would make an exhibition of herself in the town: singing, dancing and throwing her clothes off. Ordinarily she was a quiet, shy, sensitive, very respectable housewife from a good local family, living with her husband and two school-age children in a charming semi-detached house on a pleasant estate. She and all the family had to live with the knowledge of what had happened a number of times, could well happen again with little warning; and that a lot of people knew about it.

Axiom II: help individual members of the family with their feelings

In addition to those associated with the adaptive process, a range of feelings may be experienced:

1. *Bewilderment*. Especially in the early stages, families are likely to be bewildered by the sufferer's symptoms; having been told the diagnosis, the family may be little better off (Kuipers and Bebbington, 1982). This will probably be their first experience of mental illness and even if they have heard the word 'schizophrenia', for example, they will have little idea what it means beyond the notion popularised by myth and media that it involves a split personality, half of which, like Mr Hyde, is likely to be dangerous. Additionally, they are going through processes and experiences that are quite new to them, especially if a hospital admission is involved: legalities and dealings with complex institutions with a wide range of different staff.

    Apart from acknowledging people's feelings, what is needed is solid information (Hatfield, 1990). While there is still much we do not know about the causes of mental illness, there is much we can explain: what the diagnosis means, the symptomatology, the possible course of the condition and the possible prognosis. We will also need to go through the treatment being currently implemented and some of the possible options for the future. Talking about the part the different personnel are playing and introducing them will help people to understand how the team operates. All this will not be a one-off: people may well need to be told many times over. As matters progress the different stages may need some of the same handling. It needs a continuous effort from the professionals to remember that what is familiar to them almost to the point of routine is happening to others for the first time.

Another sort of bewilderment concerns people's inconsistent feelings. More likely to occur later in the process, at the heart of them is ambivalence: wanting to care but resentful of the demands this makes; wanting to discharge their responsibilities but angry that they get little appreciation, from the sufferer or others. Moods can swing, from optimism when the signs are hopeful to tiredness and despair when, with setbacks, they begin to wonder where it will all end. These mixed, fluctuating reactions can leave people confused as to what they really feel or want.

2. *Uncertainty*. As has already been mentioned, people are uncertain. They can never feel quite sure how the sufferer will be from hour to hour, day to day, or week to week. They may be on tenterhooks for much of the time, with the sufferer's behaviour a primary determinant of what sort of a time they will have. They may be free to do little without making elaborate arrangements to ensure the situation is covered, be it a matter of a few hours or a couple of weeks to give them a much needed break.

These shorter-term uncertainties are compounded by the longer-term unpredictabilities: not knowing what the eventual outcome will be. We can usually cope with the prospect of a longish period of stress, provided we have a reasonable assurance that there is some 'light at the end of the tunnel'. For people caring for those with a chronic mental illness, this reassurance is seldom possible (Mace and Rabins, 1999). For them the extra worry creeps in of what is to happen when we/I can no longer provide care. An elderly spouse with the day-to-day care of a partner with Alzheimer's disease; a pensioner daughter with 24-hour responsibility for an 85-year-old mother with the same condition; and a retired parent looking after a middle-aged son disabled by a long-standing schizophrenic condition – all share these feelings. While the eventual prospect may be the death of the dementia sufferer, this is not a means of relief welcome to the carer. For them there is no ultimate success.

3. *Guilt*. Feelings are going to be exacerbated if guilt is also involved. We have already mentioned the guilt which looks back, regretting the unkindness, intolerance, neglect, missed opportunities, insensitivity or overprotection of earlier days (whether the self-recrimination is justified or not). There is also the guilt to the effect: 'if only I had picked up the signals earlier and done something about them quicker, all this might never have happened'. Then there are the daily kinds of guilt: I can do so little to ameliorate his/her suffering; I did the wrong thing and upset them; I hate my own bad feelings which led me to take it out on them when they can't help being ill. Should feelings have tipped over into physical violence, the self-recrimination is likely to be worse and indicative of an approaching breaking-point.

People can even feel guilty about being ashamed of having mental illness in the family. There is still enough misunderstanding, stigma and discrimination against people with a history of mental illness (Birch, 1983) to make families choose to shelter the sufferer; but at the same time they feel as though they were letting the sufferer down by not sticking up for them in the public arena and, in effect, colluding with such attitudes rather than challenging them.

> Mrs R. was the wife of an (ex-) manager of a local branch of a bank. He had developed a pre-senile dementia in his fifties, became coarse, vulgar, foul-tempered, ill-mannered, dishevelled and was totally without insight. He remained physically fit and active, however. Their two children were now married and settled in careers in other parts of the country. The bank had retired him early and there were no particular financial worries. Apart from feeling that her husband required almost constant supervision, his wife felt she could take him nowhere, and they had both completely dropped out of a previously extensive social circle. She had been looking forward to sharing a full life with her husband after his retirement; now she had only years of increasing difficulty and isolation to contemplate.

4. *Mourning*. Besides mourning the loved one they have 'lost', people may need to mourn for what they themselves have lost or resigned.

Quite apart from the financial hardship which caring almost invariably entails, plans, hopes, perhaps dreams for themselves have to be laid aside.

5. *Anger*. Involved here are the feelings people may have about what they are (or are not) getting from the professional services. Families have complained (Hatfield and Lefley, 1987) that professionals are remote, inaccessible when needed, talk theoretical jargon and are really only concerned with the patient. They have little time for the family's anxieties, play them down, show little appreciation of what the family is contributing and generally disparage it. What they sometimes are offered is family therapy which implies the illness is somehow their fault. What they look for is information, advice and practical services. Unless we are sensitive to families they will manage their difficulties as best they can with whatever help they can find elsewhere. As second best, this can only be detrimental to them, to what we are trying to achieve and, crucially, to the sufferer.

Responding to feelings

For me, the method of choice in responding to these issues of the feelings of individual members of the family would be good casework. It is in this area of practice that, for example, Biestek's principles (1961) and Hollis' analysis of methodology (1972) still have much to say. I know the elevation of casework into some sort of mystique needed bringing down to earth (Fischer, 1977), but the denigration of casework and caseworkers in the revolutionary days of the late 1960s (for example, by *Casecon* magazine) was equally unbalanced. Since then a range of new methods of working have become available to social work practitioners: behaviour modification (Hudson and Macdonald, 1986), family group therapy (Barnes, 1984; Minuchin, 1977), transactional analysis (Pitman, 1984), task-centred practice (Reid and Epstein, 1972), cognitive therapy (Wills and Sanders, 1997; Alford and Beck, 1998) cognitive-behavioural therapy (Dobson, 1995) personal construct psychology (Winter, 1994), a variety of types of groupwork (Preston-Shoot, 1987), community work (Twelvetrees, 1982) and community social work (Hadley *et al.*, 1987) among them. There have also been attempts to bring all social work methods together into comprehensive unitary approaches (Pincus and

Minahan, 1973; Middleman and Goldberg, 1974; Goldstein, 1973; Siporin, 1975; Whittaker, 1974; Coulshed, 1991; Evans and Kearney, 1996; Payne, 1997; Parton and O'Byrne, 2000). It is to be hoped that we have learned to discriminate and recognise that particular methods are at their best in particular situations to deal with a certain range of problems, with none a cure-all. Just what can be done with good casework in mental health is chronicled by Oliver, Huxter and Butler (1990).

One of my concerns is the possibility that, in future, the priorities for British social work practice will become child protection work, organising practical packages of care for people with disabilities, and the supervision of offenders in the community. While these are valid tasks to undertake on behalf of society which call for new skills, some of the old skills of listening, following and responding to what people are telling us could become peripheral to mainstream practice and marginalised to specialist voluntary agencies. Should this happen, many people's needs will go unmet. Helping people to deal with their feelings in work with families with a mentally ill member could become one of the casualties of such a change.

Children

To end the exploration of this axiom, a crucial point should be made. We have been discussing the impact of bewilderment, loss, grief, uncertainty, ambivalence, guilt, shame, embarrassment, pressure and the lack of appropriate help as though these were happening to adults. It has been suggested above that even well-functioning adults are not going to have an easy time of it. What then must be the effects on young children if one of their parents becomes ill? They can be devastated. The well parent will have the enormous task of trying to meet the extra needs of the children at a time when they are trying to cope with both parental roles and to support the ill spouse. A one-parent family could be shattered. The obvious social work task is to help the well partner (or support the substitute parent) and we reassure ourselves that by helping the parent we are helping the children. This may be true or it can be a rationalisation. We can be all too conscious of the strength of the children's needs (Elliot and Place, 1998) and fear that, should we try to address them, we would be overwhelmed by them if we once 'took the cork out of the bottle'.

Child abuse work has taught us to look at the needs of children and to try to respond to them with forms of therapy. The children of families where there is mental illness merit our help just as much as any other child at risk of severe damage. They rarely seem to be considered for such help at the time they most need it, assuming that the facilities exist, that is. The implications for their futures are, sadly, obvious.

Axiom III: help families with their management strategies

By management is meant the day-to-day ways in which families cope with their situation, not management in the commercial sense, with its overtones of organising and subordinating people. How to manage is a constant source of worry to families and they look to the professionals for advice on this subject more frequently than any other. Two broad areas are involved: the management of relations with the ill person and the family's management of their own lives, though these are obviously closely interlinked. Much of what has already been written has a bearing. An effective treatment programme will reduce the amount of 'illness' to be managed; when people as a team know what they are working towards, uncertainty is reduced and management issues are clearer. Although we discussed the creation of an appropriate environment predominantly from the point of view of meeting the needs of the sufferer, this can obviously help to relieve the pressure of managing on the family too. The services brought in or to which the sufferer goes out will help families, since others will be sharing responsibilities with them. Information, advice, helping them through process stages and to deal with their own feelings – these will all contribute to both areas of the managing process. There are three particular aspects to be expanded upon here: reactions to symptoms, consistency and families' own lives.

Reactions to symptomatology

Research suggests that families find it more difficult to cope with the negative symptoms of psychosis than with the positive (Wing and Creer, 1975; Watkins, 1996). The positive symptoms are the active symptoms such as hallucinations, delusions, excitement, overt despair, disorientation, aggressiveness and hostility, disturbed sleep patterns, damage to property, resisting treatment, or socially offensive and embarrassing behaviour. Negative symptoms are those related to passivity: moodiness, withdrawal, isolation, blunted feelings giving the impression of indifference, the 'glass wall' shutting-out of others, the vacant stare, lethargy, self-neglect (poor appetite, poor appearance, scruffy clothing), lack of personal hygiene (unwashed, unshaved, unkempt) and incontinence.

While coping with positive symptoms can be hard, they have certain merits in terms of the management involved:

1. They are clearly illness-related and in that sense are forgivable; the sufferer is not culpable.
2. They come at you and therefore give something to work with.
3. They largely call for a response of control, so people know what they are trying to achieve, even if the choice of means remains open.
4. If their own efforts to control fail, families have a clear and legitimate reason for calling in reinforcements, informal or formal. They can do so without feeling guilty and assured that others will share their objective – the restoration of control.

Negative symptoms do not have the same quality:

1. They are not so clearly illness-related, so the issue of culpability is not so clear-cut. The uncertainty about how to respond leaves family members more uncomfortable and anxious.
2. With negative symptoms the initiative has to come from the family, the response from the sufferer. It always takes a much more sustained effort to keep an initiative going, especially when there is little in the way of response or change.
3. The ends are more complex. With negative symptoms we are trying to stimulate some kind of response, not merely control. If the ends are more complex, so are the means, adding to the management issues.
4. There is less legitimacy in calling in others, since the complaint is of absence rather than presence: what is not rather than what is. The people brought in will be asking, 'What do you want me to do? What can I do about it?' What the family might be wanting to say is 'Give them a good ticking-off/shake them up/make them be

what we would like them to be.' These are not practicable answers to the questions, though, and the family probably know it, reflecting their frustration.

As professionals we know the most difficult clients to deal with are the unresponsive. At least we can try to be objective about this and not take it personally; while at the end of the day we can put work aside and take up our personal lives. Such escape routes are not available to families. They live with the situation rather than visit it, and it is hard to be objective when enmeshed in deeply significant relationships which have a past, a present and an ongoing future. Families do not have the luxury of being able to close cases and send the papers for filing. This is their personal life; if they have an escape at all it is into their working lives. Their experience and ours are not the same thing.

Management consistency

If any management strategy is to succeed it needs to be sufficiently consistent in four respects:

1. *It must be sufficiently consistent with the needs of the situation.* Self-evidently, if there is a mismatch between needs and strategies a breakdown is inevitable at some point. The needs to be considered are those of the family as well as those of the sufferer. Consistency is not to be confused with rigidity; as situations develop and change, management will need to adapt. Successful consistency has to have flexibility.
2. *It must be sufficiently consistent over time.* While acknowledging the need for flexibility, there is a vast difference between this and vacillation: switching round between firmness and indulgence, involvement and disassociation, so that no-one knows where they stand or what is expected of them. This sort of confusion can only aggravate tensions and make any sort of management more difficult.
3. *There must be sufficient consistency between the various members of the family.* Anything else will be confusing to the person with the illness or enable them to manipulate others, playing one off against another. Neither alternative is healthy. Family differences may be about the approach broadly, but the arguments are likely

to be presented as specifics, such as what to be firm about and what to let pass: appearance, manners, getting up, going out, taking risks, and so on. These differences will reflect not only general tolerance levels, for example, but also what members think is important and what trivial. Some values may be rational and arguable and are not likely to cause real trouble; others have an irrational tinge or possess a particular symbolism – they touch off charged emotions and are the more likely to produce rows and bad feelings.

4. *Management strategy must be sufficiently consistent with what any professionals are doing.* If the staff at the day centre, say, have a programme of firmness in certain matters, indulging them at home is not going to help achieve the ends in view. Overprotection at home can stifle the progress that day-centre staff may have made in self-management. We need an agreed programme in both spheres, with the professionals recognising that the family have a great deal of experience, knowing what is or is not likely to work with this member. The family will also have ideas about what they can or cannot achieve in their sphere – at least as a starting-point. With help they may be able to achieve more than they thought originally, perhaps by professionals introducing them to new techniques.

Management techniques are many and varied, from bribery to coercion. In between we may encourage and support what people are doing, endorse what they propose, make suggestions of our own, offer advice, caution against, try to deter or resort to sanctions – withdrawal of privileges, pleasures, rewards or affection. Choosing a method will be a matter of assessing which is likely to be the more effective in the long run, but bearing in mind the general principle that rewarding behaviour you want to encourage works more effectively than trying to deter behaviour you wish to discourage.

As a technique, behaviour modification has developed this area of practice in a more structured way than many others. Hudson (1978) examines its value in working with schizophrenia sufferers. For some, this calculated way of managing behaviour smacks too much of manipulation. Protagonists of the technique would argue that in everyday social life we are constantly rewarding or discouraging by smiling, frowning, tone of voice or subtle body language – means of communication of which we may be barely conscious. To look at what we are doing and make conscious choices about it is more rather than less ethical, they would suggest.

Basically, we are here looking at the way people communicate with each other and to what effect. There are a number of approaches to this, transactional analysis being perhaps the most systematic. Clarifying what is happening in communication should help us to identify where any problems lie and to assist their resolution by providing suggestions for more productive problem-solving techniques. This sort of framework has been used in approaches to reducing high EE, for example (Falloon and Pederson, 1985).

Helping families to live their own lives

Unless we do this where necessary, families will be unable to go on caring for the sufferer in the longer term. A breakdown would generally be a disaster for the sufferer and mean a bleaker prognosis; the social worker would be faced with a much more difficult task; the agency might have to shoulder the costs of substitute care; and the family would have the guilt of failure to bear. However, the better reason for helping is that people have a right to their own lives: they are not there just to be someone else's carer and a convenient substitute for public services. Fundamentally they have the right to choose to care or not. Though people may accept the Hobson's choice of caring if that is all they are offered, theirs will be a grudging service of dubious quality. Other families may want to choose to care, but if the prospect is one of being left to struggle on their own they may decide not to try. Enabling choice is the aim of helping here. What people freely choose will produce the commitment and quality of care that accompanies it, to the sufferer's benefit.

To help families live their lives in the way they would choose as continuing carers, there are three broad ways professionals can assist: giving support, providing practical services and linking them to other sources of support:

1. *Offering professional support*. For families, this means our being there when they need us. We should be able to respond quickly, to deliver the services they may need when they need them, in a way which is acceptable to them. The availability of this sort of back-up would give families the security and confidence to main-

tain their caring. This has profound implications for the way we organise our services; it suggests a round-the-clock availability of a locally-based centre where a sufficiently wide range of resources is at the disposal of a multidisciplinary team – a kind of fourth standby service in addition to police, ambulance and fire services.

2. *Providing practical services.* These should be geared to families' needs. If they also benefit the sufferer that is a bonus, but not the rationale for providing them. Perhaps the most significant of services is respite care (McCullough, 1989) – anything from a couple of hours to all day, all night, a weekend, a fortnight or three months; anything from 'sitting' to alternating care. Not only does respite provide a break from the onus of caring, it also means that members of the family have some chance to preserve a life of their own. Buying a new outfit, visiting the hairdresser, a coffee morning with friends, an evening out at the club, an adult education class, a hobby or interest group, a weekend with relatives, the chance to get to family occasions such as a wedding, a holiday – these are the sort of opportunities we ordinarily get to maintain social contacts, keep satisfying relationships alive and pursue self-realisation.

There are a variety of other services which, one way or another, can help to ease the pressures: a laundry service to help cope with incontinence; the district nurse calling to help prevent complications such as bed sores; home helps and family aides to assist with household matters; someone to deal with the occasional household repairs, look after the garden, and so on. With these tasks and worries taken care of, more time and energy can go elsewhere.

3. *Putting families in touch with other support systems.* Here we are primarily thinking of links with other people facing the same difficulties. While we can do this under the aegis of public services through professionally sponsored support groups, it is probably better if we can connect families to a voluntary organisation. Many families value belonging to one as an alternative source of information of all kinds: the nature of the illness, its treatment, the latest research findings and service developments; legislation and its ramifications from rights under the Mental Health Act to the latest changes in social security provisions. Such organisations are also providers of much practical advice based on members' experience, while many offer practical services or will support representations to public providers. Their specialised knowledge of the relevant civil and welfare rights and wholehearted

commitment to sufferers and families equips them to get more effective results in their tangles with officialdom than we might do. As professionals we are part of that officialdom and in an equivocal position.

Perhaps the most valuable function of voluntary organisations, though, is to help break down the sense of isolation that families so often feel: that this is happening to us alone and there is no-one who really understands what we are going through. To share experiences with others who are or who have been in a similar position can be an enormous relief, especially in confirming the normality of the confusion of feelings and reactions families have. They are given permission, particularly, to have the negative feelings of anger, resentment, sorrow and despair that as 'good' carers (kind, tolerant, patient, cheerful, optimistic) others do not let them express ordinarily. Families fear that, if they do express them, they will be seen as 'bad' carers. Their peers give them the right to think of themselves and put the needs of the sufferer into a more realistic perspective.

A voluntary organisation is not always the answer, however. Some families will not link up, basically because they are still rejecting the identification that joining would imply. A shared experience does not guarantee that people are going to get along with each other; a local branch may not match the needs of a particular family. For the most part what voluntary organisations offer are varieties of groupwork, and at their best meet needs that individual casework is not equipped to meet. It seems regrettable that group work has had an uphill fight for recognition as a valid fieldwork method in many agencies, which has left staff to promote groups in their 'spare' time: not the best of auguries.

Axiom IV: help resolve maladaptive patterns

Coping patterns were mentioned earlier, and here some ideas about them are developed. Some patterns will be dysfunctional; that is, they are not in the best long-term interests of the sufferer, the family or both and will need to be addressed. Even if for the moment they appear to be working, they could be building up tensions since in the final analysis they function at the expense of someone who cannot go on paying the price for ever. A proportion of the dysfunctional patterns can reasonably easily be dealt with, since they are based on misinformation, misapprehensions, misperceptions or misunderstandings which can be resolved on a rational basis. Some are going to be harder to change since strong, perhaps unrecognised, even unconscious, feelings are involved.

The advent of mental illness in a family is obviously going to disturb not just the patterns of daily living and hopes and aspirations for the future, but also the way in which emotional needs are met and satisfactions achieved. The degree of disturbance will clearly vary with the significance of the relationship involved. A son-in-law may be distressed that his mother-in-law is developing a dementia, but, as she is probably not a primary figure in his life in the way that his wife, children and parents are, he is unlikely to be profoundly upset, even if he is considerably involved in the practicalities of her care. More significant for him might be his wife's reactions to her mother's illness. While he would support her in her caring efforts, should she become so totally absorbed in that care that she emotionally neglected him, he would become considerably affected. A young wife depressed after the birth of a child, a young husband developing paranoid ideas, an only child becoming floridly ill with schizophrenia in late adolescence – these are going to produce a deep disturbance in the distribution of needs, the ways in which they are met, and in sources of satisfaction. The giving and taking of nurture, affection, responsibility, authority and sexuality can be radically changed, while the consequent technicalities of child care, running the home, looking after the garden, seeing to the car, paying the bills and so on produce unfamiliar stresses which can only add to the emotional disruption. The new situation will produce new priorities – perhaps changes in leadership and dependency, new balances in weighing risk and caution, sociability and privateness, initiatives and habits or technical skills.

Patterns of response

Unhelpful responses to circumstances may fall into different patterns:

1. People may resign themselves to what they have. As a short-term strategy this works, but in the longer term the strain tells: needs and satisfactions cannot be resigned for ever.

2. People find alternative ways of getting needs met and other sources of satisfaction within family life, but almost invariably at a cost to someone else. Father misses being looked after by his wife and 'promotes' his eldest daughter into the role, however unwelcome she finds it.

3. People look outside for what they are missing and the family splits. A husband looks for sexual gratification elsewhere as his depressed wife has no desire. There is a higher incidence of divorce in families where there is a mental illness.

4. Rather differently, there is the rare occasion where a mental illness shifts matters in a way which better suits one or more members of the family, providing a source of gratification, an important secondary gain or a new strength to a collusive alliance. Sustaining these involves destructively perpetuating the illness A couple may enjoy becoming 'parents' again, recapturing a role and meaning to life they had missed once their children had grown up, but this could be at the expense of someone who needed to re-enter adult life.

Such patterns will need to be dealt with; but we need to be sure first that any patterns we tackle are dysfunctional. To illustrate this point I go back to the patterns distinguished in Chapter 6. Diagrammatically they might be represented as in Figure 7.1. Each pattern shown will have its particular mix of attitudes, feelings, tensions and means of managing. Indeed it is from these elements that we will begin to identify which of the patterns is tending to predominate, One further factor contributing to our understanding is the way the family make use of professional help. Do they get in touch readily or reluctantly; do they ask for constructive assistance or only want someone to listen to their complaints; do they respond to advice or ignore it; are they trying to manipulate professionals into a 'big stick' or other kinds of role; are they saying, in effect, this is now your problem and we are having no more to do with it; or are they saying we will take care of things without your interference and are breaking off contact?

In this regard, two caveats apply: first, that what is overtly expressed in the family may not always be consistent with the covert messages being sent. We may need time and sensitivity before we pick up what is really happening at the different levels. Second, that families who complain often have every right to do so in the light of the service they are getting. The anger they direct at us can be perfectly reasonable and not a sign of dysfunction elsewhere. For us to assume it is a defensive ploy on their part (such as projection) can be a defensive ploy of our own. Psychoanalytic approaches can seductively offer explanations which put the fault on the client rather than the therapist.

Figure 7.1 *Patterns of response*

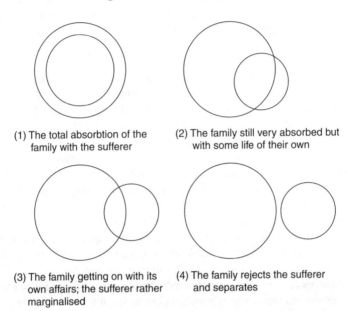

(1) The total absorbtion of the family with the sufferer

(2) The family still very absorbed but with some life of their own

(3) The family getting on with its own affairs; the sufferer rather marginalised

(4) The family rejects the sufferer and separates

Functionality or dysfunctionality of patterns

Of the four patterns outlined in Figure 7.1, (1) is arguably functional as a short-term response to acute crisis, but thereafter dysfunctional since it does not allow for growth and change in either sufferer or family. There are two possible qualifications to this:

(i) If we accept the analytic explanations of say, schizophrenia, to heal the personality could require a regression to an infant state where this degree of absorption would be justified for some time as a precursor to healthier growth by reparenting through the developmental stages. For the family of origin to be able to handle this is rare: too much has happened over too long a period. Parent substitution by the therapist is more commonly used. However,

Winnicott has been heard to advocate the use of regression/ recovery in child guidance work and the parents have managed this with his help.

(ii) This degree of absorption could be required in, for example, the final stages of a dementia where the sufferer may become as functionally helpless as a young child. The dysfunctionality would occur if the inordinate demands were to be carried by only one person.

Pattern (4) is usually highly dysfunctional for the sufferer. To face life with no support from family is a daunting prospect for the most mature of us, let alone those who have been through a mental illness. Also, the totally isolated client is the most difficult for the social worker to help. About the only circumstance in which a sufferer would be better off away from family is where they are unchangeably making matters worse for the sufferer, as with an unalterably 'high EE' family. Even here, keeping some links, however tenuous, would afford benefits: the rejection would not be entire. To reject the ill member could be functional for the family if this was the only way it could survive; though this suggests the family already has considerable problems of its own. The demands of care can sometimes tax the resources of even the most capable families, however.

Patterns (2) and (3) are potentially functional and sustainable on a longer-term basis, though with incipient strains. In (2) the family could be struggling somewhat to maintain this level of care and perhaps perpetuating dependency. In (3) it would be the ill person who felt threatened by his/her somewhat tenuous membership of the family, with dependency needs unmet. What we might have in mind as an aim is a kind of '2½': a sufficient meeting of the needs of both family and sufferer.

Addressing dysfunctional elements

These simplified patterns imply a rather rare consistency of approach by all the family members over time. It is more likely that the dysfunctional elements are partial, involve some family members, leaving others unhappy about matters but at least potential cooperators with, say, a family therapist trying to challenge and change what was happening. They are inconsistent families, if they can be called that in a positive sense. By way of illustrating what is meant using a structural approach to the family dynamics and the archetypal family of four, a diagrammatic representation of their usual functioning might look like that shown in Figure 7.2.

Figure 7.2   *The (western) cultural assumption*

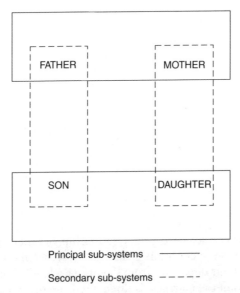

Principal sub-systems   ————

Secondary sub-systems — — — —

Let us assume that both children are in their 'teens and that the son develops a schizophrenic illness. There are now possibilities for dysfunctional patterns approximating each of the four types but involving only some of the family. In the first case (Figure 7.3, p. 130), mother feels so guilty she has preferred her daughter that she over-compensates and becomes totally immersed in the care of the son. In this new structural picture, father and daughter have lost or become excluded from their principal sub-systems and it is uncertain which way any secondary sub-systems will develop. If father/mother develop at least a secondary one and daughter maintains one with her brother and/or mother, or develops one with father, the family could survive on a 'lesser of two evils' basis. The risk of a split is real, since the usual patterns of meeting needs and finding satisfactions have been disrupted. Father and daughter could start looking elsewhere, isolating mother and son still further in an unhealthy tie. It would not be unreasonable to assume that father and daughter would be seeking to salvage the family's life for some time before they decided to write it off and would back attempts to restore a healthier pattern.

Figure 7.3   *Dysfunctional scenario 1*

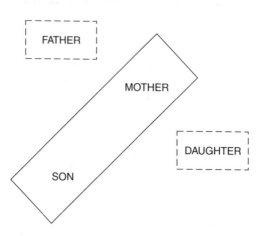

In the second scenario, the relationship between mother and father has largely been built around the care of the children. As adolescents, their departure from the primary family is looming and thus the basis of the marriage is threatened. Neither parent wants to face this issue and the illness of the son provides them with the chance to go on parenting him and so keeping the marriage together. The structure now looks like that shown in Figure 7.4. Father and mother preserve a life for themselves but by incorporating the son into their primary sub-system. Again this is unhealthy for him and jeopardises the daughter's position unless she can establish a secondary sub-system with someone to remain in some contact.

In the third scenario, father and mother find it hard to accept the son's illness. Father especially had invested much in his son's future success as a vehicle for dealing vicariously with his own feelings of failure. He transfers his investment to his daughter, joining mother in this. The daughter, jealous of the son's position for many years, is ready to concur in the new alliances. The new structure appears as in Figure 7.5. The son's position is now tenuous; while father and mother will continue to provide for him out of a sense of parental

Figure 7.4 *Dysfunctional scenario 2*

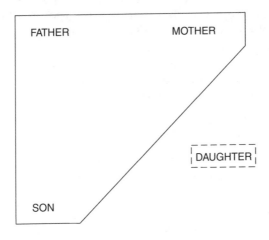

Figure 7.5 *Dysfunctional scenario 3*

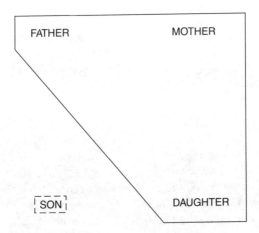

responsibility, he badly needs at least a secondary sub-system if he is not to be completely isolated.

In the fourth scenario, the 'well' members of the family have a vested interest in living together without the 'ill' member obtruding. His existence is effectively denied since it represents more of a threat than the others can tolerate. The nature of the experienced threat may vary among the family members. Father and mother, say, share a common repressed fear of their own 'badness'. The son's illness stirs this fear and they have to resort to crisis defensive strategies to deal with it, collusively projecting their fears onto the son and shutting him out of their lives. The daughter, heavily dependent on her parents, fears the loss of them if she does not do the same and allies herself with them. The son's situation is now desperate (see Figure 7.6) – he is now no longer even a sub-system.

Figure 7.6   *Dysfunctional scenario 4*

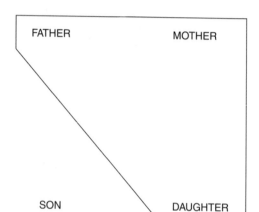

These hypothetical examples are simplistic in some respects: for example a dementia is likely to involve a three-generation family rather than the two described. Only a small percentage of the situations with which we become involved are likely to throw up issues of this kind, but we are bound to come across them from time to time. On occasion I began to wonder if something was afoot when plans we had all worked out and agreed hit snags which stalled them, even though the explanations given for the hold-ups were rational. I became more convinced when this happened a number of times and assumed the form of a pattern rather than just coincidence or bad luck. I am not joining the 'it's all the family's fault' lobby, but just occasionally, in working for the sufferer, we reach the point where we have to decide, in everyone's interests, whether to try to tackle what is going on under the surface in family dynamics or accept it as immutable and try to get round it. The decision will depend on our evaluation of the 'workability' available in the personalities and interactions extant; and a consideration of which approach – family therapy, transactional analysis or behaviour modification, for example – would be the most likely to yield results. At stake would be the prevention of damaging or potentially disastrous outcomes in the future.

Although in this chapter I have overtly used a traditional Western family model, I consider the approach has a cross-cultural validity. While other cultures would produce different patterns, their functionality or dysfunctionality would still need to be considered in the same sort of way. In whatever way we become involved, however, working with families is a vital area of practice. We neglect it at high cost – to them, to us, to agencies and, most importantly, to the sufferer.

Conclusion

There is little doubt in my own mind that the quality of mental health emergency and statutory social work has vastly improved over the years even if it took the stimulus of an Act of Parliament to achieve it by creating the approved social worker (ASW) role and training for it. Largely gone are the days of the kind of horror story I used to get from some of my students. Recruited green to a local authority social services department, they were automatically made mental welfare officers and put on the duty rota after only six weeks' experience in the department and no training whatsoever. Acknowledging that they were hopelessly out of their depth, they nevertheless had to struggle with the issues of life and liberty which then confronted them.

Whether there has been the same degree of improvement in longer-term work is more doubtful. Fisher, Newton and Sainsbury (1984) found no identifiable rationale as to why some sufferers received a long-term intervention and others only a brief, crisis-oriented service in what appeared to be similar circumstances. This suggests in some instances the social workers were possibly wasting their time by prolonging contacts unnecessarily, while in others they were failing to meet the needs that existed. More profoundly, the discussion whether or not the functions of the approved social worker should be extended to other mental health personnel has called into question the future shape of social work practice in this crucial sphere.

In an interesting correspondence in *Professional Social Work*. August/September 2000, two very different scenarios emerged. Dr Ramon Shulamit, as a psychiatrist, wanted to see social workers liberate themselves from what he saw as the narrow statutory confines of the ASW role and contribute with other mental health professions to the tremendous amount and variety of work that still needed to be done if users were get a quality service. By contrast, Roger Hargreaves saw the retention of the ASW role as essential, not just as a civil liber-ties safeguard through the involvement of a professional from a different organisation and allegiance, but as a base for mental health social work practice. Without that formal base he was concerned that social workers would ultimately be elbowed out by the more powerful medical professions and organisation. Without a specific practitioner and with social work functions scattered among professionals with other primary concerns, there was every chance social work would disappear from the mental health services altogether to the detriment of everyone, not least users. Personally, I do not see why the ASW role *per se* should be a constraint. I cannot recall any of my old mental welfare officer colleagues being inhibited by their powers of compulsion, or their ASW successors. A much more likely constraint is the lack of resources – especially time – which turns statutory work into the top priority. How this issue is finally resolved, only (considerable) time will tell

In this book, by identifying what might need to be done, I hope I have demonstrated what can be done and in the process helped to dispel the feeling that mental health social work is hopeless and hardly worth trying. Even if we cannot yet cure the illness, good social work can make a great deal of difference to the quality of life of sufferers, their families and carers; and at times it can make the difference between life and death.

Bibliography

Abel, K. *et al.* (eds) (1996) *Planning Community Mental Health Services for Women*, London, Routledge.

Alford, B. and Beck, A. (1998) *The Integrative Power of Cognitive Therapy*, New York, Guilford Press.

Arksey, H., Hepworth, D. and Quereshi, H. (1998) *Carers' Needs and the Carers Act*, York, York University Social Policy Unit.

Atkinson, S. (1993) *Climbing out of Depression*, Oxford, Lion Publishing.

Banks, N. (1999) *White Counsellors, Black Clients*, Aldershot, Ashgate.

Barham, P. and Hayward, R. (1991) *From the Mental Patient to the Person*, London, Routledge/Tavistock.

Barker, P.J. and Baldwin, S. (eds) (1991) *Ethical Issues in Mental Health*, London, Chapman & Hall.

Barker, P., Campbell, P. and Davidson, B. (eds) (1999) *From the Ashes of Experience*, London, Whurr Publishers.

Barker, P. and Davidson, B. (1998) *Ethical Strife*, London, Arnold.

Barnes, G.G. (1984) *Working with Families*, London, Macmillan – now Palgrave.

Barnes, M. and Berke, J. (1990) *Mary Barnes: Two Accounts of a Journey through Madness*, London, Free Association.

Barnes, M. and Maple, N. (1992) *Women and Mental Health: Challenging the Sterotypes*, Birmingham, Venture Press.

Bartlett, H. (1970) *The Common Base of Social Work Practice*, New York, National Association of Social Workers.

Barton, R. (1959) *Institutional Neurosis*, Guildford, John Wright.

Bellack, A. *et al.* (1997) *Social Skills Training for Schizophrenia*, New York, Guilford Press.

Bernlef, J. (1988) *Out of Mind*, London, Faber.

Bhugra, D. and Bahl, V. (1999) *Ethnicity: An Agenda for Mental Health*, London, Gaskell.

Biestek, F.P. (1961) *The Casework Relationship*, London, Allen & Unwin.

Birch, A. (1983) *What Chance Have We Got?*, Manchester, Manchester MIND.

Bornat, J., Johnson, J., Pereira, C., Pilgrim, D. and Williams, F. (1997) *Community Care: A Reader* (2nd edn) London, Macmillan/Open University.

Brandon, D. (1991) *Consumer Power in Psychiatric Services*, London, Macmillan – now Palgrave.

Brearley, C.P. (1982) *Risk in Social Work*, London, Routledge & Kegan Paul.

Breggin, P. (1993) *Toxic Psychiatry: A Psychiatrist Speaks Out*, London, HarperCollins.

British Association of Social Workers (1996) *The Code of Ethics for Social Work*, Birmingham, BASW.

Brown, G.W. and Harris, T. (1979) *Social Origins of Depression*, London, Tavistock.

Brown, G.W., Birley, J.L.T. and Wing, J.K. (1972) 'Influence of Family Life on the Course of Schizophrenic Disorders', *British Journal of Psychiatry*, vol. 121, pp. 241–58.

Bryant, M. (2000) 'Serving the Need Inside', *Professional Social Work*, August, p. 8, Birmingham.

CCETSW (1976) *Values in Social Work*, Paper 13, London, Central Council for Education and Training in Social Work.

Charleworth, E. and Nathan, R. (1997) *Stress Management: A Comprehensive Guide to Wellness*, London, Souvenir Press.

Chamberlin, J. (1988) *On our Own*, London, MIND.

Clare, A. (1976) *Psychiatry in Dissent*, London, Tavistock.

Clark, C. (1999) *Social Work Ethics: Politics, Principles and Practice*, London, Macmillan – now Palgrave.

Clark, C. and Asquith, S. (1985) *Social Work and Social Philosophy*, London, Tavistock.

CMH (1981) *Principles of Normalisation*, London, Campaign for Mental Handicap.

CNA (1992) *Speak Up, Speak Out*, London, Carers National Association.

Cohen, D. (ed.) (1990) 'Challenging the Therapeutic State', *Journal of Mind and Behaviour* (special issue).

Coulshed, V. (1991) *Social Work Practice*, London, BASW/ Macmillan – now Palgrave.

Crepaz-Keay, D., Binns, C. and Wilson, E. (1997) *Dancing with Angels*, London, Central Council for Education and Training in Social Work.

Crichton, J. (1995) *Psychiatric Patient Violence: Risk and Response*, London, Duckworth.

Curtis Report (1946) *The Report of the Care of Children Committee*, Cmd 6922, London, HMSO.

Dawson, C. and McDonald, A. (2000) 'Assessing Mental Capacity', *Practice*, vol. 2, no. 2.

Day, P. (1981) *Social Work and Social Control*, London, Tavistock.

Deacon, S. (1992) 'It is Chris's Illness but We All Have the Scars', *The Independent*, 2 January.

Dobson, K. (ed.) (1995) *Handbook of Cognitive Behavioural Therapies*, New York, Guilford.

Department of Health (1990) *The Care Programme Approach*, HC 90/23/ LASSL, London, HMSO.

—— (1993) *The Health of the Nation: Key Area Handbook, Mental Health*, 3/ 93 0/N 14914/A, London, HMSO.

—— (1994) *Advocacy – a Code of Practice*, UK Advocacy Network, F54/017 1804, London, HMSO.

—— (1995) *Building Bridges*, London, HMSO.

—— (1997) *Developing Partnership in Mental Health*, Cm 3555, London, HMSO.

—— (1998) *Our Healthier Nation: A Contract for Health*, Cm 3852, London, HMSO.

—— (1999) *Review of the Mental Health Act, 1983*, Report of the Expert Committee (Chair: Richardson, Genevra), London, HMSO.

—— (1999) *Reform of the Mental Health Act 1983*, Cm 4480, London, HMSO.

—— (l999) *National Service Framework*, 1999/0572, London, HMSO.

—— (2000) *The NHS Plan – a plan for investment*, Cm 4818-l, London, HMSO.

—— (2001) *Reforming the Mental Health Act*, Cm 5016/I, London, HMSO.

Dunn, C. (1998) *Ethical Issues in Mental Illness*, Aldershot, Ashgate.

Dunn, S. (1999) *Creating Accepting Communities*, London, MIND.

Elliot, J. and Place, M. (1998) *Children in Difficulty: A Guide to Understanding and Helping*, London, Routledge.

Evans, D. and Kearney, J. (1996) *Working in Social Care: A Sytemic Approach*, Aldershot, Arena.

Eysenck, H.J. (1975) *The Future of Psychiatry*, London, Methuen.

Falloon, J.R.H. and Pederson, J. (1985) 'Family Management in the Prevention of Morbidity of Schizophrenia: Adjustment of the Family Unit', *British Journal of Psychiatry*, vol. 147, pp. 156–63.

Fennel, M. (1999) *Overcoming Low Self-esteem*, London, Robinson.

Fernando, S. (1995) *Mental Health in a Multi-Ethnic Society*, London, Routledge.

Fischer, J. (1977) *Effective Casework Practice*, New York, McGraw-Hill.

Fisher, M., Newton, C. and Sainsbury, E. (1984) *Mental Health Social Work Observed*, London, Allen & Unwin.

Fontana, D. (1999) *Meditation: An Introductory Guide to Relaxation for Mind and Body*, Shaftesbury, Element.

Galloway, J. (1990) *The Trick is to Keep Breathing*, London, Minerva.

Goffman, E. (1968) *Asylums*, Harmondsworth, Penguin.

Goldsmith, M. (1996) *Hearing the Voices of People with Dementia: Opportunities and Obstacles*, London, Jessica Kingsley Publications.

Goldstein, H. (1973) *Social Work Practice: A Unitary Approach*, Columbia, University of South Carolina Press.

Good, V. (1989) 'Speak, Listen, Learn and Help', *Social Work Today*, 4 May, vol. 20, pp. 18–19.

Goodwin, S. (1990) *Community Care and the Future of Mental Health Service Provision*, Aldershot, Avebury.

Gostin, L. (1975) *A Human Condition*, London, MIND.

Grant, L. (1998) *Remind Me Who I am Again*, London, Granta.

Hadley, R., Cooper, M., Dale, P. and Stacey, G. (1987) *Community Worker's Handbook*, London, Routledge.

Hatfield, A. (1990) *Family Education in Mental Illness*, New York, Guilford Press.

Hatfield, A. and Lefley, H. (eds) (1987) *Families of the Mentally Ill*, London, Cassell.

Hawton, K., Simkin, S., Malmberg, A., Fagg, J. and Harris, L. (1998) *Suicide and Stress in Farmers*, London, Stationery Office Books.

Heller, T., Reynolds, J., Gomm, R., Muston, R. and Pattison, S. (1996) *Mental Health Matters*, London, Macmillan/Open University.

Heron, C. (1998) *Working with Carers*, London, Jessica Kingsley Publications.

Hershenson, D.B. and Power, P.W. (1987) *Mental Health Counselling: Theory and Practice*, New York, Pergamon.

Hollis, F. (1972) *Casework: A Psycho-Social Therapy*, New York, Random House.

Howard, B. (1988) 'Mania', *Openmind*, no. 35, p. 11.

Howe, G. (1997) *Serious Mental Illness – a Family Affair*, London, Sheldon Press.

Howe, G. (1998) *Getting Into the System – Living with Serious Mental Illness*, London, Jessica Kingsley Publications.

Hudson, B.L. (1978) 'Behavioural Social Work with Schizophrenic Patients', *British Journal of Social Work*, vol. 8, no. 2, pp. 159–70.

Hudson, B.L. and Macdonald, G.M. (1986) *Behavioural Social Work: An Introduction*, London, Macmillan – now Palgrave.

Hutten, J. (1977) *Short-term Contracts in Social Work*, London, Routledge & Kegan Paul.

Huxley, A. (1977) *Doors of Perception*, London, Panther.

Illich, I. (1977) *Limits to Medicine*, Harmondsworth, Penguin.

Jahoda, M. (1958) *Current Concepts of Positive Mental Health*, New York, Basic Books.

Jenkinson, P. (1988) 'Owning Up to Racism in a Multi-Racial Society', *Social Work Today*, 29 September, vol. 20, no. 5, pp. 20–1.

Johnstone, L. (1988) *Users and Abusers of Psychiatry: A Critical Look at Traditional Psychiatric Practice*, London, Routledge.

Kemshall, H. and Pritchard, J. (eds) (1997) *Good Practice in Risk Assessment and Risk Management* (vols. I and II), London, Jessica Kingsley Publications.

Kennerly, H. (1997) *Overcoming Anxiety*, London, Robinson.

Klein, J. (1960) Birmingham University lectures.

Kuipers, L. and Bebbington, P. (1982) *Living with Mental Illness*, London, Souvenir/Mental Health Foundation.

Kutchins, H. and Kirk, S. (1999) *Making Us Crazy*, London, Constable.

Lacey, R. (1996) *The Complete Guide to Psychiatric Drugs: A Layman's Guide* (2nd edn), London, Embury Press.

Laing, R.D. (1970) *The Divided Self*, Harmondsworth, Penguin.

Lamb, H.R. and associates (1976) *Community Survival for Long Term Patients*, San Francisco, Jossey-Bass.

Langan, J. (1999) 'Assessing Risk in Mental Health', in P. Parsloe (ed.), *Risk Assessment in Social Care*, London, Jessica Kingsley Publications.

Lawless, J. (1998) *Aroma Therapy and the Mind*, London, Thorsons.

Leff, J., Kuipers, L., Berkowitz, R., Eberlein-Vries, R. and Sturgeon, D. (1982) 'A Controlled Trial of Social Intervention in the Families of Schizophrenic Patients', *British Journal of Psychiatry*, vol. 141, pp. 121–34.

Leslie, A. (1991) *Victims of Confusion: Case Studies of Elderly Sufferers from Confusion and Dementia*, London, Jessica Kingsley.

Lewis, J. and Meredith, B. (1988) *Daughters Who Care*, London, Routledge.

Lindenfeld, G. (1993) *Managing Anger*, London, Thorsons.

Littlewood, R. and Lipsedge, M. (1997) *Aliens and Alienists: Ethnic Minorities and Psychiatry*, London, Hutchinson.

Lowe, A. (1988) 'Patients' Groups Change Mental Health Service', *Social Work Today*, 4 August, vol. 19, no. 48, pp. 16–17.

Mace, N.L. and Rabins, P. (1999) *The 36 hour Day* (2nd edn), Liverpool, Johns Hopkins University Press.

Maslow, A. (1969) *Toward a Psychology of Being*, London, Van Nostrand Reinhold.

McCormick, E.W. (1997) *Surviving Breakdown*, London, Vermilion.

McCullogh, J.W. and Prins, H.A. (1978) *Signs of Stress*, London, Woburn.

McCullough, D. (1989) 'The Hidden Army's Weakest Flank', *Social Work Today*, 12 October, vol. 21, no. 7, pp. 18–19.

McDonald, A. (1999) *Understanding Community Care: A Guide for Social Workers*, London, Macmillan – now Palgrave.

Meacher, M. (1972) *Taken for a Ride*, London, Longman.

MHAC (1992) *Fourth Biennial Report 1989–91*, Mental Health Act Commission, London, HMSO.

MHF (1998) *Healing Minds*, London, Mental Health Foundation.

Middleman, R. and Goldberg, G. (1974) *Social Service Delivery – a Structural Approach*, Columbia, Columbia University Press.

Mills, E. (1962) *Living with Mental Illness*, London, Routledge & Kegan Paul.

MIND (1995) *A–Z of Complementary and Alternative Therapies*, London, MIND.

MIND (2000) *Mind Millenium Awards 1997–2000*, London, MIND.

Minuchin, S. (1977) *Families and Family Therapy*, New York, Routledge.

Mitchell, J. (ed.) (1986) *Selected Melanie Klein*, Harmondsworth, Penguin.

Mitchell, S. (1999) *Massage: Introductory Guide to the Healing Power of Touch*, Shaftesbury, Element.

Morris, J. (2000) *Community Care – Working in Partnership with Service Users*, Birmingham, Venture Press.

Morris, T. and P. (1963) *Pentonville: A Sociological Study of an English Prison*, London, Routledge & Kegan Paul.

NACRO (1998) *Risks and Rights – Mentally Disturbed Offenders and Public Protection*, London, Mental Health Advisory Committee, NACRO.

Neale, R.M. (1998) *To Challenge or not to Challenge*, Kelso, Curlew Productions.

NSF (1973) *Schizophrenia, the Family Burden*, Surbiton, National Schizophrenia Fellowship.

Oliver, J.P.J., Huxter, P.J. and Butler, A. (1990) *Mental Health Casework: Illuminations and Reflections*, Manchester, Manchester University Press.

Open Mind (2000) no. 101, Jan./Feb. Special Edition on Risk.

Palmer, S. (ed.) (1999) *Counselling in a Multi-cultural Society*, London, Sage.

Parish, A. (1998) *Volunteers and Mental Health Befriending*, London, National Centre for Volunteering.

Parker, C. and McCullocgh, A. (1999) *Key Issues from Homicide Enquiries*, London, MIND.

Parsloe, P. (1999) *Pathways to Empowerment*, Birmingham, Venture Press.

Parton, N. and O'Byrne, D. (2000) *Constructive Social Work – Towards a New Practice*, London, Macmillan – now Palgrave.

Patmore, C. and Weaver, T. (1991) *Community Mental Health Teams: Lessons for Planners and Managers*, London, Good Practices in Mental Health.

Payne, M. (1997) *Modern Social Work Theory*, London, Macmillan – now Palgrave.

Payne, M. (2000) *Teamwork in Multi-professional Care*, London, Macmillan – now Palgrave.

Pedler, M. (1999) *Mind the Law: Evidence to the Mental Health Act Review Team*, London, MIND.

Perlman, H. (1957) *Social Casework: A Problem Solving Process*, Chicago, Chicago University Press.

Philo, G., Henderson L. and McLaughlin, G. (1993) *Mass Media Representation of Mental Health/Illness*, Report for Health Education Board for Scotland, Glasgow University Media Group.

Pilgrim, D. and Rogers, A. (1999) *A Sociology of Mental Health and Illnes* (3rd edn), Milton Keynes, Open University Press.

Pincus, A. and Minahan, A. (1973) *Social Work Practice: Model and Method*, Itasca, Peacock Publications.

Pink, F.G. (1990) 'Yours Sincerely, F.G. Pink', *Guardian Society*, 11 April.

Pitman, E. (1984) *Transactional Analysis for Social Workers and Counsellors*, London, Routledge & Kegan Paul.

Plant, R. (1970) *Social and Moral Theory and Casework*, London, Routledge & Kegan Paul.

Preston-Shoot, M. (1987) *Effective Groupwork*, London, Macmillan – now Palgrave.

Prins, H. (1986) 'Social Work and the Mentally Disordered: Towards Empathetic Understanding', in *Skills for the Eighties*, Birmingham, British Association of Social Workers.

Prins, H. (1995) *Offenders, Deviants or Patients?* London, Routledge.

Prins, H. (1999) *Will They Do It Again?* London, Routledge.

Pritchard, C. (1995) *Suicide: The Ultimate Rejection*, Milton Keynes, Open University Press.

Pulling, J. (1987) *The Caring Trap*, London, Fontana.

Rack, P. (1982) *Race, Culture and Mental Disorder*, London, Tavistock.

Ramon, S. (1988) 'Leaving Hospital', *Openmind*, no. 34, pp. 12–14.

Rayner, J. (2001) 'Mad Remedies', *Observer*, 7 January.

Read, J. and Wallcraft, J. (1995) *Guidelines on Advocacy in Mental Health Work*, London, UNISON/MIND.

Reed, J. and Baker, S. (1996) *Not Just Sticks and Stones*, London, MIND.

Rees, S. (1978) *Social Work Face to Face*, London, Edward Arnold.

Rees, S. and Wallace, A. (1982) *Verdicts on Social Work*, London, Edward Arnold.

Reid W. and Epstein, L. (1972) *Task Centred Casework*, New York, Columbia University Press.

Rhodes, M.L. (1986) *Ethical Dilemmas in Social Work Practice*, Boston, Routledge & Kegan Paul.

Ritchie, J., Dick, D. and Graham, R. (1994) *Report into the Care and Treatment of Christopher Clunis*, North East and South East Thames Regional Health Authorities, Dept of Health, London, HMSO.

Rogers, A., Pilgrim D. and Lacey, R. (1993) *Experiencing Psychiatry*, London, MIND/Macmillan – now Palgrave.

Rogers, J., Came, M., Romilly-Pitts, K. and Furness, J. (1989) *Outside, Inside*, London, Outsider Publications.

Rollin, H. (ed.) (1983) *Coping with Schizophrenia*, London, Hutchinson.

Romme, M. and Escher, S. (1993) *Accepting Voices*, London, MIND.

Rose, D. (2001) *Users' Voices*, London, Sainsbury Centre for Mental Health.

Rowe, D. (1988) *The Experience of Depression*, London, Fontana.

Rowe, D. (1996) *Depression – the Way Out of your Prison*, London, Routledge.

Sainsbury, E., Nixon, S. and Phillips, D. (1982) *Social Work in Focus*, London, Routledge & Kegan Paul.

Sartre, J.-P. (1969) *Being and Nothingness*, London, Methuen.

Sayce, L. (1990) *Waiting for Community Care*, London, MIND.

Sayce, L. (2000) *From Psychiatric Patient to Citizen*, London, Macmillan – now Palgrave.

Seed, P. (1988) *Towards Independent Living: Issues for Different Client Groups*, London, Jessica Kingsley Publications.

Seed, P. (1989) *Introducing Network Analysis in Social Work*, London, Jessica Kingsley Publications.

Sheppard, M. (1990) *Mental Health – the Role of the Approved Social Worker*, Sheffield, Joint Unit for Social Services Research, Social Services Monographs: Research in Practice Series, University of Sheffield.

Sheppard, M. (1991) 'Approved Social Work – Walking the Tightrope', in *Community Care*, 28 November.

Sheppard, M. (1991) 'General Practice, Social Work and Mental Health Sections: The Social Control of Women', *British Journal of Social Work*, vol. 21, no. 6, pp. 663–83.

Shorter, E. (1997) *A History of Psychiatry: From the Era of the Asylum to the Age of Prozac*, London, Wiley.

Siegler, M. and Osmond, H. (1966) 'Models of Madness', *British Journal of Psychiatry*, vol. 112, pp. 1193–203.

Silove, D. and Manicavasagar, V. (1997) *Overcoming Panic*, London, Robinson.

Siporin, M. (1975) *Introduction to Social Work Practice*, New York, Collier – Macmillan.

Skynner, A.C.R. (1976) *One Flesh, Separate Persons: Principles of Family and Marital Therapy*, London, Constable.

Skynner, R. (1990) 'Judging the Mental Olympics', *The Guardian Weekend*, 13/14 January.

Smith, N. (1983) *Mental Disorder: What You Should Know*, Croydon, Greenway Press.

Stein, L. and Santos, A. (1998) *Aggressive Community Treatment of Persons with a Severe Mental Illness*, New York, W.W. Norton.

Styron, W. (1991) *Darkness Visible*, London, Cape.

Surma, J. (1991) *Community Care is a Woman's Issue*, Coventry, University of Warwick Social Care Practice Centre.

Szasz, T.S. (1961) *The Myth of Mental Illness*, New York, Hoeber-Harper.

Taylor, R.D.W., Huxley, P.J. and Johnson, D.A.W. (1984) 'The Role of Social Networks in the Maintenance of Schizophrenic Patients', *British Journal of Social Work*, vol. 14, no. 2, pp. 129–40.

Tielveit, A. (1999) *Ethics and Values in Psychotherapy*, New York, Routledge.

Townsend, P. (1962) *The Last refuge*, London, Routledge & Kegan Paul.

Townsend, P., Davidson, N. and Whitehead, M. (1988) *Inequalities in Health*, Harmondsworth, Penguin.

Trickett, S. (1998) *Coming off Tranquilisers, Sleeping Pills and Anti-depressants*, London, Thorsons.

Twelvetrees, A. (1982) *Community Work*, London, Macmillan – now Palgrave.

Tyrer, P., Harrison-Read, P. and Van Horn, E. (1997) *Drug Treatment in Psychiatry: A Guide for the Community Mental Health Worker*, London, Butterworth-Heinemann.

Ungerson, C. (1991) *Policy is Personal: Sex, Gender and Informal Care*, London, Tavistock.

Vaillant, G. (1970) *Adaptation to Life*, Denver, Little.

Varma, V. (ed.) (1997) *Managing Manic Depressive Disorders*, London, Jessica Kingsley Publications.

Vaughan, C.E. and Leff, J.P. (1976) 'The Influence of the Family and Social Factors on the Course of Psychiatric Illness', *British Journal of Psychiatry*, vol. 129, pp. 125–37.

Watkins, J. (1996) *Living with Schizophrenia: An Holistic Approach*, Melbourne, Hill of Content.

Whittaker, J.K. (1974) *Social Treatment: An Approach to Inter-personal Helping*, New York, Aldine.

Wilcock, G. (1990) *Living with Alzheimer's Disease*, Harmondsworth, Penguin.

Wills, F. and Sanders D. (1997) *Cognitive Therapy: Transforming the Image*, London, Sage.

Wilson, J. and Myers, J. (1998) *Self Help Groups* (2nd edn) Sherwood, R.A. Wilson.

Wing, J.K. (1978) *Reasoning about Madness*, Oxford, Oxford University Press.

Wing, J.K. (ed.) (1983) 'Schizophrenia From Within', in H. Rollin (ed.), *Coping with Schizophrenia*, London, Hutchinson.

Wing, J.K. and Creer, C. (1975) *Schizophrenia at Home*, Surbiton, National Schizophrenia Fellowship.

Winnicott, D.W. (1964) 'The Value of Depression', *British Journal of Psychiatric Social Work*, vol. 7, no. 3.

Winter, D. (1994) *Personal Construct Psychology and Clinical Practice*, London, Routledge.

Woodall, R. (1992) 'Why My Son Went to Live in a Cave', *The Independent*, 7 April.

Zgola, J. (1999) *Care that Works: A Relationship Approach to Persons with Dementia*, Liverpool, Johns Hopkins University Press.

Zito Trust (1993) *Learning the Lessons*, London, Zito Trust.

Index